Dear Jean

Dear Jean

What They Don't Teach You at the Water Cooler

Jean Kelley

Atwood Publishing
TULSA, OKLAHOMA

Dedication

To my family, my friends, my staff,
and the thousands of clients
who have passed through my life.
All my experiences both negative and positive
have given me rich material for this book.

Contents

AVAILABLE SEPARATELY IN PAMPHLET/REPORT FORM
Dear Jean Career Advice

- Preparing to Look
  - —I'm Going Back to School
  - —Know What You Want
- Crafting a Cover Letter and Resume
  - —I Need a Decent Resume
  - —Choppy Job Record
  - —Can I Cover a Break in My Work Record?
- Looking For A Job
  - —Will They Find Me a Job?
  - —I've Never Used an Agency
  - —Responding to Recruiting
- The Importance of the Interview
  - —Go It Alone When Interviewing
  - —Late to an Interview
- Do You Really Want *This* Job?
  - —You Can't Afford This Job
  - —No Travel, Please
  - —They Asked for My Age
- You May Not Get the Job
  - —I Thought I Had the Job
  - —Criminal Record Keeps Me from Getting a Job
  - —It Might Have Been Slander   ·
  - —He Didn't Give Me a Reference

- Raises and Evaluations
  - —My Husband Needs a Raise
  - —When Can I Ask for a Raise?
  - —How to Request a Raise
  - —When Should I Get an Evaluation?
- Career Changes and Changes at Work
  - —I Hate the Constant Changes
  - —Returning to Work
  - —Replacement Boss
  - —Should I Keep This Job?
  - —Should I Wait Around?
  - —No More Hours
  - —There's Not Enough To Do
- How Do You Know When It's Time To Move On?
  - —Move On Down the Road
  - —Should I Wait Until It's Posted?
- How To Leave Your Job
  - —How Much Notice Should I Give?
  - —Leaving a Bad Situation
- Find Out Why You Were Fired
  - —Fired and I Don't Know Why
  - —They Should Know What Happened
  - —Temporary Temporaries

To order see form on back page

List of Letters

Wired and Wireless

Parties, Lunches, and Dinners

Giving and Receiving

Best Bosses Finish First

Foreword

T

he Remarkable Jean Kelley" is the title bestowed by her business associates on the author of the book you are about to read. "Remarkable" means "worthy of notice...extraordinary." Both are excellent descriptions of this unusual woman. Jean's climb from a checkered high school career into a highly respected member of the Tulsa community is a magnificent and inspirational story. Here is a woman who, in her 20s, was addicted to alcohol and found herself living a fast life headed toward self-destruction. With the help of friends, she turned her life around.

Jean created and operates a successful business that survives recessions and prospers in the face of strong local and national competition. She has twice been elected to the Chamber of Commerce Board of Directors and was named Woman Entrepreneur of the Year by that esteemed organization. Jean has been showered with awards galore for her many community services. She now writes a business column and appears regularly on radio and television, providing practical advice on how to succeed in business. This once challenging and rebellious student at Daniel Webster High School is a recent addition to that institution's Hall of Fame. Jean did not head off to college with the rest of her class, yet she is now a postgraduate student at Harvard Business School. In addition to her flourishing career, Jean is a loving and caring wife, daughter, stepmother and friend.

Jean says her life is another story for another time. This may be true, but it's important for you to know that the book you are about to read is written by a woman who has fought the same battles you are fighting, struggled with the same questions that paralyze you, and has overcome them. You are fortunate to have "the Remarkable Jean Kelley" to help you with your own quest.

—DON REYNOLDS, AUTHOR
CrackerJack Positioning

Acknowledgments

My heartfelt thanks to. . .

My loving partner in life, Bill, who probably wondered early on if this book was a pipe dream, and who must have wished he had a nickel for every time he heard the words "the book." Bill, thanks for not saying "are you ever going to finish?"

Don Reynolds, whose steady support and tireless work on his own successful book, *Crackerjack Positioning,* set the example for me to press on and finish this work. Don, thanks for many hours of advice and constant bolstering.

Kristin Stephens, my editor, friend, and member of my core staff, whose four years of midnight oil, passion, dedication, and tenacity kept me pointed in the right direction. Thank you, Kristin. Believe it or not, some of my fondest memories are of our days locked in that windowless cubbyhole with two desks, two Mac's and a printer, working toward the arrival of the book and your baby, Michael.

Margaret Wick, my dear friend and first mentor, who taught me much of what I know about living successfully on the planet and, more importantly, who is always there for me. Thank you!

Amelia Smith, special friend, whose graceful spirit always gives me a lift. Thanks, Amelia, for helping me through those dark periods and for helping me to see the beauty in everyday life.

Peggy Fielding, my friend and writing advisor, whose unfailing belief in me and many helpful hints kept me putting one foot in front of the other for the last seven years of preparation for this book. Thanks, Peggy.

Tawna Wheeler, writer and friend, who remembers me as a writer wannabe. And the Cafe Writers who cheered me along the way to completion of this project. Thanks to each of you.

The late Cavett Robert, who said to me in his southern drawl, "Jean, if you want to do something in this world, teach people how to live in it." Here's my best effort, Cavett!

A special thanks to Cindy Earnest and Susan Mount for keeping Jean Kelley Personnel running smoothly this past year while I worked nearly full time on this book.

Bob Parrish, retired psychologist, friend, and cheering section. Your faith in me helped me to be the best I can be.

Virgil Hensley, long-time friend and my teacher of goal setting. Look, Virgil, I set the **big goal** and reached it.

Thanks to Gordon Osberghaus and KOTV, Tim Van Maren, Sammy Carrillo, Mark Hyatt and KBEZ, Tim Retherford, Ralph Schaefer and the *Tulsa Business Journal.*

Dear Reader,

Because of my many years in the personnel business, people come to me for "on the job" advice. It seems that there are few, if any, resources they can turn to for advice about their workplace problems. There is a need for a book that is easily referenced and has everything in one place. This book fills that need. You might call it a mentor in paper and ink.

Dear Jean: What they Don't Teach you at the Watercooler has been designed especially for four types of people:

1. If you are in your first ten years of business life, you will find answers to your most pressing questions and ways of thinking that will accelerate your business success. Also, what you learn will promote a way of living that will enhance your personal and family life.

2. If you are a supervisor or manager, this book will provide direct guidance and help you know what your staff members think about each day. Both can dramatically increase your ability to create a productive work environment.

3. If you are the owner or manager of a small business, you will find a wealth of information about the many problems that plague small businesses. I've included most of the mistakes I've made in 24 years of running a business in the hope that you can avoid most or all of them.

4. Are you a voyeur? Do you enjoy peeking into the personal lives of others? You can read about the sticky situations others are involved in and say to yourself, "Whew! At least I'm not *that* bad."

The book is organized so that you can easily look up the answers to your own office dilemmas. The question-and-answer format is fast-moving and has a casual style. You can whiz through a chapter in no time, picking and choosing the areas that are of most interest to you.

The questions in this book are authentic, though many have been abbreviated and re-worded in the interests of space and privacy. Many of the situations in this book were called in live to me at KOTV where I am a weekly commentator on the "Six in the Morning" show. Some are letters written to me as a result of my column in the *Tulsa Business Journal*. Others were taken from my years of experience in personnel and include a wide range of workplace predicaments. If you don't see yourself in this book, you will definitely see people you know. You may even think your co-workers sent in the questions. The names have been changed, of course.

As you read, try to imagine how you would answer the questions yourself. In several cases you may say, "I knew that." There is no rocket science here, but I promise that if you use what you learn, your work life will be easier.

I encourage you to be introspective and check out your own values as you read. Not everything is black and white. For instance, what do you do when you find out your boss is cheating on her expense account? There may be more than one answer to many of these quandaries, so I hope this book will encourage you to think about what fits best with your personal values and where your loyalties lie.

You may not always agree with me. Several of my readers and listeners haven't, and a number of their letters are included. I do not claim that my way is the only way, but my assertions have been road-tested over years in business, so I'm entitled to be emphatic.

The chapters in this book will guide you in both "office etiquette" and "emotional etiquette." Office etiquette includes all those things that are just good manners and good business. In these chapters, I talk about everything from what to give your boss on Boss's Day to how to write a sympathy note. In several places I include examples of forms I use in my office. Feel free to copy and use them. "Emotional etiquette" is about taking other people's (and your own) emotions into consideration. In these chapters, I address everything from irritating co-workers to sex with your boss.

This book also includes my NOYB (None of Your Business) list. The NOYB list alone is worth the price of the book. What is **not** your business will probably shock you. For instance, if your boss is having an affair it is **not your business** unless it's with you. A lot of the things we worry about at night and talk about at work are none of our business in the first place. You can save yourself a lot of sleepless nights by etching this list onto the cortex of your brain. While you're at it, try thinking of a few more things that fall under the same category in your office — you might be surprised how many things will appear on your own list. If you are successful in marking all of these things off your "worry list," you will be close to saying goodbye to the kind of thinking that promotes ulcers, headaches, and a whole host of other depleting ailments. You'll also be a more pleasant person overall.

I hope you enjoy this book and grow from reading it. Unfortunately, I can't answer all of your questions personally, but if you have a particular question that is not covered here, e-mail or write me. Maybe I'll add it to my next book, *More Workday Wisdom*.

—JEAN KELLEY

P.S.: Take this book to work. Quote it often!

Warning-Disclaimer

This book is designed to provide information in regard to the subject matter covered. It is sold with the understanding that the publisher and author are not engaged in rendering legal advice, psychological counseling, or other professional services. If legal or other expert assistance is required, the services of a competent professional should be sought.

Every effort has been made to make this book as complete and accurate as possible. However, there may be mistakes both typographical and in content. Therefore, this text should be used only as a general guide, not as the ultimate answer to your questions.

The purpose of this book is to educate and entertain. The author and Atwood Publishing shall have neither liability nor responsibility to any person or entity with respect to any loss or damage caused, or alleged to be caused, directly or indirectly by the information contained in this book.

If you do not wish to be bound by the above, you may return this book to the author for a full refund.

Co-worker Complaints

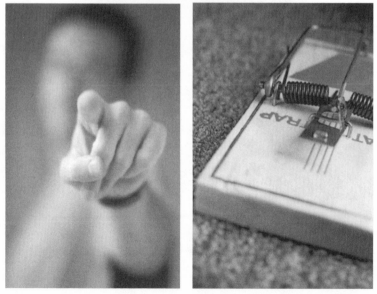

Work might actually be fun if it weren't for the people you have to work with. Think back to your last frustration. Were people involved? Unless you work at home, you will have to learn to communicate with and sometimes just put up with all sorts of people. Some will be easy to work with, some tolerable, and others will be nightmares on legs. Getting along with people is a full-time endeavor. That means if you are gainfully employed, you are really working at two jobs, not one.

There will most always be people who will cheat you, lie to you, steal from you, snitch on you, and try to get you fired. The challenge is: how to do your job well, make a good impression, and keep from getting taken advantage of by self-absorbed co-workers.

Studies show that co-worker complaints and petty turf wars keep employees stirred up more than complaints about their bosses. If the time spent gossiping about co-workers was spent on productivity, output could increase by 25 percent, maybe more. Just think, your income might increase in the same proportion.

Face it. It is just more fun to talk about people than it is to do our work. This pastime is enjoyed at the management level as much as it is enjoyed in the company at large. When we are not talking about our co-workers, we are talking about our bosses. This behavior happens at home, too. Picture yourself at home having dinner at the end of the day. If you aren't talking about your boss or your co-workers, you're probably talking about a family member who is not present — or your mouth is full. Somehow it makes us feel superior if we can see ourselves just a little smarter, better looking, or more moral than the next person.

Now about minding your own business. I accept the fact that gossip is at times more interesting than your job. But most of what we get upset about on the job is not our business. Here is a partial list of things about your co-workers or bosses that fall into the NOYB (none of your business) category. There are plenty of other things that are not your business, but I've listed nine points to avoid at all costs.

The Jean Kelley NOYB List

These things are NONE OF YOUR BUSINESS:

1. How your boss chooses to run his/her company or department
2. What your boss does with her/his at-work time
3. What your co-workers do with their at-work time
4. Whose boss or co-worker is having an affair
5. What people do before and after work
6. How people are being treated by their boss or co-workers
7. Anything derogatory about someone who is not present
8. Which employees are viewing XXX material on a company computer
9. What people eat and who weighs too much/too little

To excel as an employee, all you need to do is avoid *even thinking* about the above nine points, have a little bit of talent, and be pleasant and well-groomed. You will be surprised how fast you will whiz up the corporate ladder. Really.

Revolting Co-workers

Intraoffice strife involves putting up with the habits of others who share our space. Mood swings, gross habits, and power trips are the norm. And if that is not bad enough, we put up with ill-bred, self-centered, insensitive people who, in some cases and for whatever reason, would like to see us fired. How do we dodge the minefield? How can we stand our ground and still not alienate those we share our 8:00 A.M. to 5:00 P.M. life with? I hope you will find some of the answers here.

Let's start with co-workers who are personally disgusting. For example, have you ever pulled the short straw and had to tell a co-worker about his body odor?

My husband, Bill, told me of a co-worker of his who, week after week, wore the same shirt several days in a row. And you guessed it, no deodorant.

Even worse, this man was the payroll/personnel manager, and 175 people had contact with him every time they picked up their paychecks. Short of not getting paid, there was no way to avoid him.

There were few grievances in the summer. The thought of spending time in this fellow's unair-conditioned office was enough to keep the most cantankerous employee on the straight and narrow. My husband once told him straight out that he had B.O. You know what happened? Nothing.

This went on quite a long time until one employee got fed up. He took on this air-pollution project as a mission. Slowly and surely, he talked to everyone in the plant. Those who wanted to participate in this plan were to buy a bottle of deodorant and put it on the payroll manager's desk. Sure enough, early one August day Mr. B.O. walked into his office and was greeted by nearly 100 bottles of "armpit Dior."

You may not have had a "fragrant co-worker," but surely you have had co-workers you would like to be rid of. If they reported to you, you wouldn't feel so powerless, but they don't, so you end up with three choices. You can find a new job, accept the situation, or change your attitude.

Noisy Plumbing

Dear Jean,

The man who works next to me clears his throat incessantly. This constant ugly sound is driving me wild. What should I do, short of quitting my job?

Reply:

There is little you can do about someone else's plumbing. Mentioning this to him will be a lot like teaching a pig to sing. One, it won't work; and two, it irritates the pig.

The fact that he does this "incessantly" leads me to believe that he either has a chronic respiratory complication or just a plain old nasty habit. Short of having yourself (or the man) hypnotized, the way I see it you have three options. You can accept the behavior, you can ask to be moved to another part of the work area, or you can wear earplugs.

The Gum Chewers

Dear Jean,

A lot of my co-workers chew gum at work. They smack on it while they're on the telephone and also during intraoffice conversation. How do I politely ask them to stop?

Reply:

Politely ask them to stop.

Directness without compassion is rudeness.

Please don't misunderstand. It is surely easier said than done to approach a co-worker about a habit that is annoying to you or others.

Many people are unaware that their habits, such as smacking gum, are annoying. My last reply was not intended to sound flip. There are many situations in which being direct is the best way to handle a problem. I didn't say rude. The difference between directness and rudeness is warmth and diplomacy. The only thing that comes out of rudeness is more rudeness.

Lazy Slob

Dear Jean,

The woman who sits next to me is a lazy slob. She eats at her desk, files her nails, goes out to smoke, chats with the people in the office, or hides out in the ladies' room. She rarely does a lick of work. How can we get her to buckle down and do her work?

Reply:

By your letter, I will assume that you are not her direct supervisor, and that's too bad, because if you were, there would be something you could do about this situation.

We all (and I do include myself) from time to time feel that someone we work with is not carrying his or her share. The trouble is that worrying about something that is beyond our control and not even our business hurts our productivity.

Everyone thinks they work harder than the boss — except the boss.

She will eventually be caught. You can count on it. So unless her low productivity is directly impacting your deadlines, your energy should be used elsewhere.

More than half of the letters I receive are from people who truly believe they work harder than their co-workers. Many of those people are convinced that they work harder than their bosses, too. So if you are one of those people who believes that you work harder than anyone else in your office, you're not alone.

So far, these people have been unbearable because of their personal habits. Let's look at the other side of the coin. There are plenty of people who think they are perfect and you are the one who is screwed up. Here's a look at a person who treats others as if they are the revolting ones.

She's a Snob

Dear Jean,

I work with a person who thinks she is better than everyone else. She has even gone so far as to say out loud that the rest of us are just a bunch of idiots. What can we do?

Reply:

Look up narcissism in the dictionary. You will find her picture. There is not much you can do about a person like this. One day she will burn a bridge and discover that she's still standing on it. If you can hold out a little longer, you just might get to see this happen.

It might make us feel a little better to think that abusive people get what's coming to them. We say to ourselves, "What goes around comes around." Somehow, saying that phrase makes us feel better. The problem is that some rotten co-workers end up becoming bosses. We'll talk more about them in Chapter Eight.

Acceptable Workplace Behavior

Everyone has a different idea of what kind of behavior is acceptable in the workplace. Each company has its own culture. When our opinions of what is acceptable are radically different, it can cause a lot of discomfort. For instance, foul language, although never appropriate, is common in many offices.

> **You do not have a right to tell co-workers how to talk, but you do have the right to tell them how to talk to *you*.**

Foul Language

Dear Jean,

When you work with people who use foul language a lot, how do you handle it?

Reply:

The best way I have ever seen this handled was by a friend of mine. No matter where she was and with whom, when she heard anything distasteful she would nicely say, "Would you mind not using language like that around me? It really bothers me when I hear that kind of language." People responded immediately — and usually with an embarrassed apology. You do not have a right to tell co-workers how to talk, but you do have the right to tell them how to talk to you.

Don't "Pan" a Good Egg

Dear Jean,

What do you do when five or six co-workers try to get you into a "pan the boss" session when you think he's a pretty good egg?

Reply:

The boss will almost always find out. Take the high ground and leave the room.

Nothing positive can come about when five or six co-workers get together for the sake of gossip. All you can do is stay as far away as possible. When someone invites you to gossip and you don't want to, here is what you say: "I really don't think it's fair to talk about Suzy. She's not here to defend herself."

Earplugs Are the Answer

Dear Jean,

The woman at the desk next to me plays her radio all day. She has permission to do this. The problem is her choice of stations. I just can't stand the kind of music she plays. Must I resort to earplugs?

Reply:

If she has permission to have the radio going, I'll bet you can get permission to bring your own radio with headphones. Or better yet, maybe you can make a compromise. Ask her if you can pick the station once in a while. Does this suggestion make you nervous? What's the worst thing that could happen? Go ahead. Try it!

Fun in the President's Office

Dear Jean,

I came in Monday morning and there was this strange look to the president's office. His desk was in disarray, with wrinkled and smashed papers everywhere. Maybe I'm paranoid, but I can put 1+1+1 together and get 3. I think someone was having a little too much fun in the president's office. Do you have any suggestions on catching the culprit?

Reply:

Well, gee, how about DNA testing or a video camera? Seriously now, why don't you get back to that stack of filing in your own work area?

"Hon" Doesn't Seem Appropriate

Dear Jean,

My boss's secretary keeps calling me "Hon." I am a 35-year-old man with four children. "Hon" doesn't seem appropriate. What do you think?

Reply:

"Hon" is not appropriate business language. Even if she claims it's just a habit and she means no disrespect, it sounds disrespectful. If you have a problem with this, you need to talk with her. Tell her you are uncomfortable when she calls you "Hon" instead of using your name. If your relationship is important to her, she may learn to call you by your name, but don't expect a miracle.

What if she doesn't stop? Some people call everyone "Hon" and they are not going to stop; they have been doing it all their life. If this is the case, get used to it. Once I mentioned to an employee that I didn't like her calling me "Sweetie." She said, "That's the way I talk, and its doubtful that I'll change." She didn't change, and she happened to be one of my best producers. I got used to it.

Touchy Subjects

Disagreements in the workplace can encroach on some pretty touchy subjects. You can quickly find yourself walking on thin ice.

A Liberal among Conservatives

Dear Jean,

I work in a small management consulting firm where there are six consultants. Rarely are we ever in town at the same time, but when we are, we seem to gather in the break room early in the morning. The topic is always politics. My partners are moderate to conservative and I'm a liberal. They seem to really have fun with this and I don't. Sometimes their opinions make me so angry I can't work for the rest of the day. What do I do?

Reply:

It concerns me that a political discussion with colleagues upsets you to the point that you can't work for the rest of the day. This kind of rage is dangerous for you and the others around you. If you are not able to come to grips with your anger, don't stay in the same room during this repartee. You might remind your five conservative colleagues that you are an "endangered species" and that they would do well to allow at least one weed to flourish and blossom in their formal little garden. Rage is never a good reaction. It clogs the pipes. Lighten up.

Punished for Honesty

Dear Jean,

I'm a salesperson for a large company. I feel that my sales manager overlooks and doesn't monitor people who overexaggerate their numbers just to reach their quotas. I feel I am being punished because I am being honest. What should I do?

Reply:

It depends on your motives. Are you concerned for the welfare of the company, or are you concerned that your bonuses won't be as big as your co-workers'? If you are truly concerned for the welfare of the company, blowing the whistle is certainly an option. It does have its drawbacks; I'm sure you know what they are.

Keep your eyes on your own work.

If you are concerned about your numbers and bonuses as they compare to your co-workers', stop. There is nothing you can do about someone else's behavior on the job. Don't give much thought to telling anyone else at this point. The boss will find out sooner or later, so just keep your mind on your job and be honest in reporting your quotas.

Racial Jokes Are Embarrassing

Dear Jean,

My best friend works for a bunch of good ol' boys. She runs the office and is the only woman in the company. I think these good ol' boys are a bunch of racists. Not a week goes by without her telling me about a racial joke she heard at work. My friend is a good-spirited person, but she becomes very nervous when the racial jokes escalate. Her husband is black. She is in desperate need of her job. A car accident left her husband in pretty bad shape. His disability is running out. My friend asked me if she should go to her boss and tell him that she is in a mixed-race marriage before someone finds out. She feels that her boss will be real embarrassed when he finds out.

Reply:

Who your friend is married to should be of no consequence to her boss or to any of the "good ol' boys" she works with, but that's not reality. If her boss has a shred of decency, he will be embarrassed when he finds out, and *he **will** find out if she continues to work there. It will be better if he finds out through your friend. I'm sensitive to your friend's fear, but the longer she hides this fact, the deeper the hole gets.*

He Keeps Saying It

Dear Jean,

I've turned in a supervisor for sexual harassment. I wrote a letter, and in it I mentioned the name of another co-worker who had said some things, too. Now, every time that co-worker says something off-color to me, he makes a face and says, "Oh, are you going to turn me in for sexual harassment?" What can I do to get him to stop saying this to me all the time?

Reply:

Every time he says, "Are you going to turn me in for sexual harassment?" reply with, "Only if you harass me."

He Harassed Me

Dear Jean,

I work at a grocery store and there is a stocker who sexually harassed me. He was given a warning and is still working here. Is there anything I can do?

Reply:

If you have reported this and it is still happening, you have three choices — handle it by yourself, quit, or report the incident to the Equal Employment Opportunity Commission. If you really like where you work, I strongly suggest that you first try to handle this yourself.

The next time he harasses you, tell him to stop it. Be sure to call his attention to what it is that he is doing. Say something like, "You are sexually harassing me, and I want you to stop." If he does it again, repeat the phrase. Unless this guy is living in La-La Land, he will know what the words sexual harassment mean. Based on the current business climate, he should also be somewhat familiar with the ultimate consequences.

By your letter, I don't know exactly what sexual harassment means to you. If this harassment is verbal, the above applies. On the other hand, if the harassment is physical, you won't want to give this creep another chance. Call the Equal Employment Opportunity Commission today.

What Can You Live With in the Workplace?

Most differences in opinion aren't that drastic. They involve what people can and cannot live with in their place of employment.

Allergic to Smoke

Dear Jean,

I work at a job where we are in one large, sectioned-off room. Several people in this area smoke, including the owner of the business. I am highly allergic to smoke, and I have told them about it and they try to stay on the other end. But it still gets to me and bothers me.

Reply:

This is really unfortunate, because if the owner smokes, there is precious little you can do about it. I guess you have done what you can do. Since you are really allergic to it, that leaves you with only one choice. If you can't accept it and you can't change it, you've got to remove yourself from the situation.

Bourbon Breath

Dear Jean,

One of my co-workers comes to work with alcohol on his breath. In fact, his breath can curl nose hairs. How should I handle this? I would just bet the boss doesn't know about his drinking. What do you think I should do?

Reply:

If your boss works in the same location as you, my guess is the secret is already out. Anything this obvious to you is probably obvious to many people in your office. If you are working on projects together and the employee's work is impaired, you may want to talk to him about how he has dropped the ball, but unless he is jeopardizing the health or safety of his fellow workers or the public, his breath is not your business.

Personal Space

A couple of years ago, I read an article about violence in relationship to personal space. According to the theory presented, the closer people are jammed together, the more violent they become. Most of us have our own desks, or at least some measure of personal space that we call our own at work. When this personal space is invaded, it leaves us feeling, well, invaded.

Privacy in a Bull Pen

Dear Jean,

I work in a large area where there are several desks and no partitions. One of my co-workers has no concept of privacy and keeps picking up things off my desk while I'm talking on the phone. About once a week, she goes through my things after I've left the office. This is a continuing annoyance. Are there any rules for privacy in a bull-pen area?

Reply:

Yes, there are. Your desk drawers are your territory and are to be considered private to anyone in your work area. You need to make it perfectly clear to this invader that you will honor her space and you want her to honor yours. There is nothing else you can do short of ratting on her to your boss. Resist the urge to put a mousetrap in your drawer.

Cubicle Confidentiality

Dear Jean,

One of my co-workers comes into my cubicle and breaks her neck straining to read my desk calendar and anything else that is on my desk. I don't want to create a scene, but what should I do short of that?

Reply:

I have had several questions this past couple of years relating to cubicle confidentiality. As you indicate, making a scene would not be to your benefit. But for this behavior to stop, you will have to take the initiative. It's best for you to bring this subject up when you are calm.

A straightforward approach would sound something like, "I feel uncomfortable when you come into my office and look over my desk. If you will tell me what you are looking for, I will help you look."

If you are uncomfortable bringing that much attention to the issue, you may want to use an indirect approach. This will take more time to accomplish the same result, but it will work equally well. Every time she visually peruses your desk, just smile nicely and say, "Are you looking for something? Maybe I can help you find it." After she hears that same question from you three or four times, she'll get the picture.

What if it is not just our personal space, but our very own body that is not treated privately?

How's the Little Father?

Dear Jean,

One of the partners in our firm is pregnant and everyone is acting like they don't see her getting rounder each week. She weighs only about 100 pounds, so I'm sure this isn't normal weight gain. She won't bring up the subject and neither will anyone else. This all seems a little odd to me. When my wife, a middle manager at a utilities company, was pregnant, everyone knew.

Reply:

Some executives are more private in regard to their pregnancies than others. They don't want their bodies or their babies to be the first comment of every business conversation. Whatever her reasons are, it's important that you respect her boundaries.

> **There is something about being pregnant that causes people to think they can walk up and try to feel the baby kick.**

There is something about being pregnant that causes people to think they can walk up and try to feel the baby kick. It's almost as though the woman's body doesn't belong to her any longer. As thrilled as they are about her upcoming arrival, some female executives are reluctant to allow tummy touching and "oohs" and "ahhs" to go on in the office.

Typically, when a couple is expecting, friends and associates will make remarks to the woman like, "How's the little mother?" They rarely say, "How's the little father?" There is nothing inherently wrong with these remarks, but some female executives prefer to stick to business during office hours.

I can tell by your question that you really care about this woman. When you are 100 percent sure she is pregnant, it would be especially nice for you to privately acknowledge that fact. A warm, enthusiastic note of support and congratulations would be in order.

Tension in the Office

Some people invade our space and generally make the environment unpleasant through anger or moodiness. Tensions can run high in the workplace. And if you've ever had a co-worker who takes his stress out on those around him, you'll understand what the people in these questions are going through.

Explosive Co-worker

Dear Jean,

I have a co-worker who got really mad and just exploded when something that happened in the office upset her. I really don't know how to deal with her anger. Any suggestions?

Reply:

The only thing you can do is go about business as usual. There are plenty of people in the workplace who are just like your co-worker. This won't be the last time you are subjected to this type of behavior. Yelling in the office is just plain rude, and in some cases it borders on verbal abuse. There has been a lot written lately on the hostile work environment.

People who are allowed to repeatedly blow off steam in an angry manner are creating a hostile environment and should be fired, but many times they are not. Where does that leave you? That leaves you with cold reality. For your sanity, you must learn to let her outbursts roll off your back. If you are not able to do that, you will have to start packing your bags. Her behavior is not something you can control.

Co-worker with Mood Swings

Dear Jean,

My co-worker is impossible. It's her mood swings. This woman is nice one minute and the next she is biting at your heels. She acts as if everything is fine, but I hear through the grapevine that I have done something to offend her or not done something exactly as she pleases. I'm not sure I should approach her at all about this. But if I do, should I do it alone or with someone who has heard the complaints to help us straighten this out? Other co-workers and I can come to work in very good moods and leave in really bad ones because of the tension she causes. How should this be handled?

Reply:

The first thing to do is to find out if you have, in fact, done something to offend her. Make an appointment to see her in private. Be direct. Stay calm and use nonjudgmental language. One thing is for sure — judgment of any kind will escalate into a fight.

Describe the behavior you see. Ask if the behavior has anything to do with you. If it doesn't, go on about your life. If it does, make the necessary changes.

Please do not approach her with someone else who has, in your words, "heard the complaints." This is your problem.

Many people don't know how they look to others. If you can master approaching her in a nonjudgmental way every time you see this behavior, you will be doing her a big favor. Don't expect gratitude for your help in her behavior modification. She'll be sure to think she has done it all on her own.

In today's competitive workplace, you will run into people who feel that it is their right and privilege to boss everyone else, whether or not that is actually their position.

Headstrong Colleague

Dear Jean,

I work in a structured environment, and there are four of us at the same level. Of course, there is a boss above us as well. We have one individual who is headstrong and who wants to be the guy in charge. He wants to make the decisions, much to the irritation of the boss. When the boss isn't there, it's even worse.

It makes all of us uncomfortable there and even gets to the point that we have little face-offs. The boss has had to talk to him a couple of times. This has been going on for about a year now. Do you have any suggestions?

Reply:

There will always be a headstrong person in your work environment. And you will always be "having to cope."

It is important for you to separate your issues from your co-workers' issues in this challenge. Ganging up on this guy will make him even more defensive and bullheaded. If you have an issue with him, take him aside and tell him. Stay calm and cordial. The conversation you have with him will not make him change, but it will make him more aware of how he is perceived, and you will grow two feet in his estimation.

Power Trip

Dear Jean,

I've bought several flower bulbs that I'm forcing for a bit of spring color. The pot sits on a wide windowsill next to my desk. The woman who shares my office thinks my gardening efforts are a useless waste of time, and I'm left scratching my head. Does sharing an office mean compromising on an issue as small as a bulb? I don't get it. Do you?

Reply:

You may think that this issue is about gardening or even about compromising. It is not. It is about power. For whatever reason, your officemate wants to control you. Her control needs are not getting met, so she is trying to control you, and you are allowing this to upset you. Don't allow yourself to fall into her web.

The next time she "tells" you anything, smile warmly and say, "I'll take that under advisement," then the very next time she "tells" you anything, smile warmly and say, "I'll take that under advisement." After six or seven broken-record replies, she'll likely find someone else to annoy.

I guess you could always step toward her face and yell, "Back off!" at the top of your lungs every time she brought up your garden, but you would end up with a whole new set of relationship problems and very little serenity.

Mental B.O.

These types of co-workers are the most toxic and are the ones who will require you to further develop your confrontation skills. If you were raised to keep peace at any cost, you will have a challenge on your hands. It takes a lot of courage to stand up for yourself without bringing yourself down to the level of the offender.

One of the best books ever written for confrontations and verbal self-defense is called *Tongue Fu*. The author's name is Sam Horn. Her book is practical, fun to read, and there's meat on every page. When it comes to confrontations, she maintains that the actual way you say things will make or break your work relationships. This book is in softcover and it's a must.

Back Stabbers

Dear Jean,

I have a question about trying to deal with people who try to stab you in the back at work. It's really hard to deal with back stabbers at work when I'm just trying to do my job. These people were nice at first, and then I turned around and they were saying terrible things about me and sabotaging me.

Reply:

I hear this more than anything: "What do I do about back-stabbing and sabotage at work when I'm just trying to do my job?" In her book Woman to Woman 2000, *Dr. Judith Briles defines sabotage as "the erosion or destruction of your personal or professional credibility or reputation which can be administered intentionally or unintentionally through overt or covert methods." Briles also says that sabotage is not only common in the office, it is increasing at an alarming rate. Often sabotage takes the form of back-stabbing, and it can happen for a multitude of reasons. The major reason is resentment.*

The first thing to do is to find out if this person is out to get you because of a grudge. Go to the person who is doing the back-stabbing and say, "Do you have a grudge against me? Is it something I did? Is there anything we can do to get onto equal ground? I understand that you're talking about me. If there is anything I did to offend you, I need to know what it was, because I don't want to offend you again."

I know. If it were this easy, there would be a lot less hostility in the workplace. But try it. And then, try it again. At least you'll be keeping the channel of communication open.

She Plays People against Each Other

Dear Jean,

I work in an office of 23 women who work full time. We have always worked well together. We have a new floater who has been here only a couple of months. She always seems to be trying to play people against each other. This is really difficult to deal with and adds a lot of stress to a very busy workplace. What should we do?

Reply:

My first thought when I read your letter was, "Wow! Twenty-three people getting along." The law of averages has to catch up sooner or later.

Since this seems to be bothering you more than the other women, make time to have a private talk with the new floater. Tell her what behaviors you see that upset you. Warning: Tell her about her observable behavior, not what you perceive her behavior to be. Then tell her how her behavior affects you. Stay very calm.

Please make sure as you address this problem that the 22 of you don't do anything as a group. Ganging up on this new person will get you absolutely nowhere.

She Terrorizes Us

Dear Jean,

My boss doesn't care what goes on in our office. In our area, we have an employee who wakes up every morning and decides what she can do to destroy someone's day. She terrorizes her victims of choice. On top of that, we think she's stolen things, but we can't prove it. She does stuff every single day that she comes to work.

We told our boss about it and he is fully aware of what goes on, but he does absolutely nothing, even about the possible stealing. There are five of us here and every one of us has had a turn as a target.

Reply:

If you want to continue to work there, you will have to confront this issue yourself because it sounds as though your boss will not support you. I would caution you not to spread the stealing rumor unless you have proof. Without proof, your boss may think that all of you are ganging up on her. And if he thinks that all of you are spreading gossip, he will probably defend her.

On the other hand, if she is in fact stealing and acting hostile and your boss condones stealing and hostility, you are in an unsafe environment. Get out.

Disgusting co-workers are everywhere, and because they don't report to us, we can't fire them. Whether it's a lazy slob or a nasty snob, the result is the same. Many days we wish they would disappear.

If you leave the company where you work, you will get a whole new set of problems. The co-worker you find objectionable may mysteriously appear again under a different name. You'll be amazed how many times this happens. And when it does, you will have a situation similar to the one you left. The lessons that you need to learn in regard to dealing with people will continue to come up until you learn them.

You may think I believe that you shouldn't quit your job because of a co-worker. Most hassles between people result from work-style differences, so for the most part, I believe you should not leave a job based on your frustration with other people. I say this because people are going to behave the way they want to behave, not the way you or I want them to behave. The biggest challenge you will have is in determining what is worthy of a battle — what is worth your energy.

I heard a philosophy that we are all born with a certain amount of energy. And when the energy is gone, it's gone forever. Suppose for a moment that is true. What would you do? Would you continue to spend your precious energy on things that you cannot change? Probably not.

On the other hand, if you are being harassed, terrorized, or abused, leaving is the responsible thing to do. It's part of taking care of yourself. What do I mean by "taking care of yourself"? Maintaining friendships with people who are abusive or mean to you erodes your self-esteem. Pretending that you like someone who has repeatedly been abusive to you makes you feel like a phony. When your insides don't match your outsides, you pay. Your stress level increases. You are more irritable, and you run the risk of hurting the people you really care about.

Making your boundaries clear is not as easy as it sounds, but if you don't, you will most likely be taken advantage of. And what complicates this more is that if you make your boundaries clear and it really sounds like you are drawing a line in the sand, you may have a war on your hands.

For instance, if racist jokes are offensive to you and you don't tell the person who tells the jokes that you are offended, there is a good chance that you will hear them over and over. On the other hand, if you hear a racist joke and threaten or harass the person who told the joke, you have, in essence, drawn a line in the sand and you are inviting their aggression. The ideal way to handle this is to talk to the offender alone and explain calmly and honestly that you believe in a non-racist work environment. Explain that the reason you aren't laughing is because the jokes aren't funny to you. If you can carry this off with grace and ease you will have very few people problems in your life.

IMPORTANT: All people problems should be analyzed by the following rules: If you can't change it, leave. If you can't leave, accept it. In other words, change the situation, leave the situation, or accept the situation. Deciding what you can and cannot change is extremely difficult. Changing a situation is do-able. Changing people without their permission is not do-able. The truth is, we can threaten people and they might temporarily adjust their behavior. We can bribe people and they might temporarily adjust their behavior. To get a long-lasting change, though, they have to want to change.

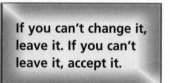

If you can't change it, leave it. If you can't leave it, accept it.

What I am saying is: the people you think you have changed have changed because they wanted to change, not because you changed them. Think about yourself. Has anyone ever made a long-lasting change in you without your permission?

Even though I have covered many points in this chapter, when you boil it all down, there are only three ways to handle co-worker dilemmas. 1. You can leave the company where you work. 2. You can change your attitudes about your co-workers. 3. You can accept your co-worker without further complaint, warts and all.

The fastest way to tranquillity in intracompany relationships is to accept life on life's terms. You will have happy, exhilarating days, and you will spend some days in the bottom of the barrel. In other words, some days will be better than others. It's not up to your boss to make it a good day for you, and it's not up to the people you work with. It's up to you to make it a good day.

Points to Remember

☐ Keep your eyes on your own work.

☐ If you can't change it, leave it. If you can't leave it, accept it.

☐ People problems in the workplace are handled best on a one-on-one basis. Develop the courage to confront your co-worker calmly. Try to resolve the problem directly before going to your boss.

☐ People don't change unless they want to.

☐ Your job is to teach people how to treat you.

☐ Take care of yourself. "Friendships" with people who are mean or abusive erode your self-esteem.

☐ It's not up to the people you work with to make it a good day for you. Only you can do that.

SEX (Shhhh!)

I f sexuality has no place in the office, why is it still in the office? Why is gossip such a global pastime?

Humans are sexual beings. There is no stopping them. And when people spend eight hours every day, day in and day out, with the same people, the topic of sex will always come up. It's human nature. Studies show that men think about sex hundreds of times per day. The numbers aren't much lower for women. We are being naive to think that all this stops when we walk into the office. Judgment is what we are after here. We must learn control.

So here we are, a large group of sexual people trying to suppress those sexual thoughts eight hours per day. Ha! The topic of sex and all related subjects will always be present in the office. Many employees even go to the office looking for their next romance.

What is accepted at one office will be grounds for dismissal at another. Larger companies are so afraid of being sued, they frown on any behavior that might be labeled provocative. I know a male manager who will not even say "You look great today" to a female.

Acting sexually demonstrative, hugging, dressing scantily, touching anywhere but on the shoulder, telling off-color jokes, and making sexual comments is risky business in today's office climate. Personally, I think this paranoia has gone way too far. I think most people have excellent judgment in this area, but the truth is, we have a wary workplace. The rules are set and we have to follow them.

Remember this NOYB (none of your business) list from the last chapter?

The Jean Kelley NOYB List

These things are NONE OF YOUR BUSINESS:

1. How your boss chooses to run his/her company or department
2. What your boss does with her/his at-work time
3. What your co-workers do with their at-work time
4. Whose boss or co-worker is having an affair
5. What people do before and after work
6. How people are being treated by their boss or co-workers
7. Anything derogatory about someone who is not present
8. Which employees are viewing XXX material on a company computer
9. What people eat and who weighs too much/too little

Look again at these. More than half of the NOYB list is about sex. Why? Because talking about who is doing what to whom is a lot more interesting than engineering, accounting, sales or information technology. Here's the rub: It's a lot riskier, too.

I'm not saying that all talk of a sexual nature will get you in deep trouble. What I am saying is that until you know exactly how your comments will be taken, it's best to not say them at all. Indulge me, please, while I say this again. Unless you know exactly how your comments will be taken, it is best not to say them at all.

Sex, gossip, and spying are just so much fun that it is hard not to get involved. I remember the day I was busted for getting involved with someone's sex life. It was back in the early '70s when a co-worker of mine, Clark, was hot for this lady named Marva. Marva was kind of a free spirit and didn't work much. Clark — the workaholic in our office — told her that she could visit him only on his lunch hour. Our boss was gone at lunchtime, and as soon as Marva walked in the door, Clark would whisk her back to his office and the fun would begin.

At first, Marva would come to visit once a week. Pretty soon she was there every day. When this whole thing started, nobody was really interested, but before too long we all stayed in at lunch to see if we could hear anything through the wall — we had to move a desk to do this.

There we were, all five of us standing against the wall, each with a glass on an ear and the glass on the wall. There was even some talk of removing the electrical outlet and rigging up a way to record what we heard.

The day our boss caught us was a dark day. She called us all into the same room and asked us to explain to Clark what we were doing and to apologize. Then she asked us to leave the room while she talked to Clark. We never saw Marva again.

I learned all my lessons the hard way. I hope you won't have to. Has one of your fellow co-workers been slurping on a manager at your annual holiday party? Is your boss having an affair? Are you getting hit on by a serial intraoffice dater? If you want to know how to handle it, it's all here. Just remember…shhhh!

Love at the Office

Intracompany dating has some risks. There are two combinations that are especially dangerous: dating your boss (or boss's boss) or dating someone who reports to you. Dating your boss is, in many cases, career suicide. You may think you can keep your rendezvous concealed, but that is nearly impossible. You may think that covert behavior, such as leaving at different times, using different elevators, and acting ultraprofessional, will seal your secret. It won't. It might help to seal your fate instead. Sooner or later, everyone will know.

As far as dating your boss goes, very few people end up married to the bosses. In companies where there is a policy against intracompany dating, someone will lose a job. It's rarely the boss.

Some years ago, I was asked to do some team building with the administrative staff of a successful company in Texas. The company wanted me to help the administrative assistants (back then they were called secretaries) of the top executives get along better with each other.

Before I accept a consulting assignment, I do an initial fact-finding session to determine if what I do fits what they need. When I did my initial visit with the staff, I was able to identify the problem immediately. Among the people I met was a beautiful young woman — we'll call her Denise — who confided to me that she was dating her boss. Her boss was the president. It wasn't necessary that she reveal this fact because her affair was not a secret. When the corporate plane left for the ski slopes, she was on it. When the corporate plane left for Mexico, she was on it.

These excursions were commonplace for this company, and the executives who worked for the company took dates on these trips, too. However, the other executives always took dates who did not work for the company. They also weren't married — unlike the president. Even worse, all the secretaries knew and liked the president's wife.

Denise complained that none of the women in the company were friendly. In some cases, they were hostile. Often, they withheld information to bottleneck her work so she would get into trouble. Believe it or not, Denise explained how depressed she was by her co-workers. She told me she felt like she was being victimized — by the secretaries, mind you, not by her boss. Naive? Yes.

I did not accept the consulting assignment, but I do know the ending of this story. It's not pretty. Upon returning from one of those trips to Mexico, Denise and her boss were greeted at the airport terminal — by the boss's wife.

Beware of the serial employee dater.

I Love my Boss

Dear Jean,

I hope you can help me. I'm in love with my unmarried boss. That's my problem. Can you help me?

Reply:

Can I help you do what? Find out if he loves you, too? Get a date? Keep your job? Find a new job? Get a divorce?

One thing is for sure, if you date your boss, your life will immediately become complicated. The bigger the company you work for, the bigger your complications will be.

Work is, at best, stressful. In some cases, it is intolerable. Unless you have a backbone of stainless steel, I suggest that you consider finding a new job before putting everything you've got into this dream. When you are securely in place at your new job, then you can, if you aren't married, begin your pursuit of your love object, your ex-boss. Happy hunting both ways.

My Boss Is Sending Her Flowers

Dear Jean,

My boss is spending a great deal of time with one of the administrative assistants in our company. They come back from lunch together, and there are flowers on her desk every couple of weeks. I'll bet they are from him.

This is getting to me because his wife might be suspicious. She is starting to ask me when he left for lunch, etc. This is stressing me out. Any suggestions?

Reply:

If what you told me are all the facts you know, you don't have enough information to make this kind of accusation. You seem to be implying that something really serious is going on. Are you positive the flowers are from your boss?

As far as his wife is concerned, you tell me that you think she is becoming suspicious. If you become sure that she is suspicious or you know for a fact that something is going on, you may then have a dilemma. Until then, it's business as usual.

In response, I got this question:

Dear Jean,

What should she do if she is sure the wife is suspicious and she knows for a fact that the boss is seeing the administrative assistant? Should she tell the wife?

My reply:

What does she have to gain by telling her boss's wife anything? She can tell his wife what she thinks she knows, and she will lose her job. For her, it would probably be a better idea to stay out of it entirely. There is no benefit to getting involved, and it really is none of her business anyway. If she is asked to lie for her boss, she will have a huge decision to make, but until then, it's back to work.

Dating across the Corporate Hierarchy

Dear Jean,

One of my employees is dating someone in the company who is higher up than I. There is no rule against this and all three of us are single, but I still feel it is an awkward situation. Is there anything I need to do to better handle this?

Reply:

Why do you feel you have to handle this? There's nothing you can do to change the situation, and the problem is inside you. I'm hoping your main concern is the quality of work produced by your staff member rather than whom she dates. Keep a close eye on her work and a blind eye on her personal life.

Gossip

Gossip is the highest form of character assassination. The thing is, we love to gossip. Office parties can bring out all kinds of sizzling talk. Within days or even hours, people have added to the original story to make it fit their personal interpretations. You have probably played the game in which people sit in a circle and you whisper something in the ear of the person sitting next to you. By the time the words get to the last person in the circle, the statement is quite different from the original. The gossip mill in the office works much the same way. There is only one good way to stay out of the gossip mill — stay out of the gossip mill.

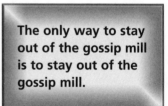

The only way to stay out of the gossip mill is to stay out of the gossip mill.

It's common knowledge that hairstylists and barbers are part-time counselors. They hear everything. People in the stylist's chair relax and unload their personal problems. The topic could be anything that is bothering them, no matter how personal.

I have been going to the same hairstylist for many years. Many of the people I know go to him as well. At no time in all the years I have known Mark have I heard him say anything bad about anyone. His behavior has fascinated me over the years, and as a result I have thrown out little tidbits of commonly known facts about people to see if he would take the bait and elaborate. He never has. So when I say "stay out of the gossip mill," I know it's possible. I've seen it done.

Ugly Gossip

Dear Jean,

I work for an accounting firm. At our annual employees-only Christmas party, my secretary and a fellow manager (also a good friend) both had way too much to drink. One thing led to another, and the next day they couldn't look each other in the eye. I'm confident that nothing will come of this, but everyone is talking about it. My secretary is single, but the manager is very married. What can I do to restore their dignity and displace this ugly gossip?

Reply:

You may want to have a discussion with your secretary spelling out the politically correct behaviors for corporate party life. Be sure to explain that what may seem innocent on her part can be gossip fodder for a whole bunch of inquiring minds. Past that, the more you stir this, the thicker it will get, and the longer it will take to calm down.

As for your friend…very married? I don't think so!

Stopping the Gossip

Dear Jean,

I am an officer of a medium-sized company. My company has a gossip problem. Somehow, one of my employees found out about my partner's mistress and has been passing rumors about it throughout the company. This information is none of their business, but it is undermining my partner's authority. What can I do to quell the rumors and get people back to work?

Reply:

Once the cat is out of the bag, there is little you can do about the gossip. Your partner was well aware of the risks when he started the affair. If you can figure out how to quell the gossip at the water cooler, let me know. I'll put it in my next book. Incidentally, if the gossip is true, it is not a rumor.

Love and My Partner's Wife

Dear Jean,

Do you answer "lonely hearts" questions? I think I'm in love with my partner's wife. We have never been alone together, but we do a lot of talking and kidding around. She is really fun to be with, and I suspect she has feelings for me, as well. She is an absolutely stunning blonde and I want her for my very own. What do you have to say about my problem?

Reply:

Wow! You do have a problem! And you also have a big decision to make. Your question indicates that your feelings for this woman may be stronger than your commitment to your partnership. I hope you will do a lot of serious contemplation before you toss your present career out the window. You are likely to find yourself without a job and without a woman.

Favoritism Because of Same Sexual Orientation

Dear Jean,

I am a middle manager in a large company. I don't really know how to explain this problem, so I'll just do my best. There is an employee of mine who is a lesbian. We work very closely, and what she doesn't know is that I am a lesbian, too. I understand her point of view so well, and I know that

I am showing her favoritism. I can't seem to help coming to her defense when people put her down because of her sexual orientation, especially when I care for her the way I do. Do you think it is wise for me to defend her? Will others be able to tell about me?

Reply:

Are you really asking me if I think it's a good idea to ask her out? The fact that you and she are lesbians has no bearing on anything. If you are displaying favoritism to anyone in your department, you are on thin ice. As far as dating an employee goes, you've been around the block. What's the best possible outcome? What's the worst?

Should I Come out of the Closet?

Dear Jean,

I am in a difficult situation. I am a very ambitious person and I am in a position where I can be promoted quickly. My prospects look very good, but it is getting harder and harder to conceal who I am from my supervisors and co-workers.

You see, I am a homosexual man. I have been in a steady relationship for eight years now and my partner is a very big part of my life. Unfortunately, though, I cannot talk about him at the office unless I "come out of the closet." Everyone thinks I am some kind of bachelor and when people get into conversations they are always asking about my personal life and trying to match me up with some female friends of theirs.

When my partner had surgery not too long ago, I had to make up a sick-relative excuse so that I could stay with him at the hospital. This is only one example, but you can imagine how difficult this is for me.

My question is, will I ruin any chances of promotion if I tell the truth? Will I damage my career? Should I just keep on living this lie? Truth is so important.

Reply:

This depends on your boss and on your company's culture. You might lose a promotion by telling the truth or you might lose a promotion by living a lie. Sooner or later, someone may find out. But maybe they won't. I know people who have lived a lie for 20 years and no one has found out. What is right for you has to fit the way you believe. If living a lie is eating you up inside, the answer is obvious.

I got several responses to this letter. Here are two that show both sides of the story.

Dear Jean,

I saw your letter about the homosexual man who wanted to come out of the closet at work. I was in sort of the same situation myself about three years ago. I took a chance and told my employer and friends at work. What a mistake! The way they treated me changed immediately. There was (for the most part) nothing I could point out as exactly different — the whole environment changed. Well, it got worse and worse and finally I ended up changing jobs and moving here. This time, I'm not telling anyone.

Dear Jean,

The sexual-discrimination climate really is getting better, by my experience. I came out of the closet at my work over a year ago and it was no problem. In fact, when I told them, they weren't even surprised. It was as if they already knew anyway. So far as I can tell, nothing has changed except that I don't feel like I'm walking on pins and needles anymore. I would encourage the person who wrote to you about coming out of the closet to come forward with the truth. It sure was worth it for me.

Sexy Past

Dear Jean,

I've gotten into politics, and I've been asked to run for mayor of my small town. As a young woman (I'm 50 now), I was a bit adventurous sexually. Do you suppose all this will come back to haunt me? What do you suggest I do?

Reply:

I don't suppose there is much you can do. It doesn't really matter whether you come from a small town or a large city, there will be a lot of people who are out to sabotage you. Sad but true, many campaigns are ruthless. If you are nimble enough to dodge the slings and arrows, go for it.

Additionally, I have known several women who have been involved in local politics who were not sexually adventurous but were branded as such. It's possible that what you did will come back to haunt you. It's also possible that many things that you did not do will haunt you as well.

None of Your Business

More than half of what people are upset about in the workplace is none of their business. That fact has never stopped them from having an opinion about it. It's human nature to have an opinion on everything, but if you want to stay afloat in the workplace, keep that opinion to yourself. Unless a particular situation directly affects your ability to make a living, it is not your business.

Kissing in Front of Me

Dear Jean,

My boss and his wife make me sick — they make all of us sick. When she visits the office, they're always kissing and draped all over each other. They stay that way until she leaves. What's wrong with these peo-ple? This is a professional office. Can't they control themselves? They have been married for 20 years. Is there anything we can do about this gross behavior?

Reply:

That may not be exactly "corporate" behavior, but he is the boss. Maybe the whole group of you should be doing your own work instead of watching and gossip-ing about your boss.

> **Unless a situation affects your ability to make a living, it's not your business.**

Married for 20 years and still that affec-tionate? The best thing you can do is congratulate them!

Here is a response:

Dear Jean,

I disagree. The boss has no business bringing his wife in and kissing all over her in a corporate office. Maybe the employees should start bringing their own spouses into the office and slobbering all over them. I bet their sloppy boss would get the hint!

My reply:

They need to chill out the gossip and heat up the work!

Love Lives at Lunch

Dear Jean,

I like to have lunch with my co-workers. Recently, the topic of conversa-tion has been their love lives. I feel uncomfortable talking about this. What should I do?

Reply:

It is not a good idea to casually talk about extremely personal things with your co-workers. If you enjoy being with these people, you may want to continue having lunch and just "pass" when this line of conversation comes up. If you feel pressured to participate, it might be good to have lunch alone for awhile. Through a strange twist of fate, you might be working for one of these people one day and you will not want your new boss to be uncomfortable with the fact that you have secret knowledge of his or her sex life.

Boss Caught Kissing

Dear Jean,

I'm a 34-year-old, happily married female in a middle-management sales position with a local company. My job requires that I travel out of town at least once a week to our various sales offices around the country.

Last week my boss and I, who is also female and married, were staying at the same hotel. I was on my way to go jogging at about 5:30 A.M. and was walking down the hallway when a door opened and a man came out. As I walked by, a woman stepped out and gave this man a big kiss.

Not only was this woman wearing only a towel, she was also my boss. Our eyes met, so I know she saw me. I think her behavior is totally disgusting, but I don't want to lose my job. What do I do?

Reply:

Nothing.

There are many situations in which the best response is no response. This is one.

Harassment

Each day, there are fewer companies that will tolerate off-color language at work. In companies where there is a great deal of cultural diversity, you will find even less tolerance for this type of pastime.

Off-color Jokes

Dear Jean,

I'm a senior manager at a large oil company. Last week, I walked into our finance department and the secretary told several of the managers and me a seriously off-color joke. I was embarrassed and angry. Should I tell the head of the department?

Reply:

Although her behavior was offensive, it is best not to make a scene after the fact. As far as telling her boss, I wouldn't. Who knows, her boss may find this amusing or entertaining. As for you, the next time she starts a story, leave the room immediately. There is no need to explain your position — you've just made it known. If the woman says, "Want to hear a good joke?" answer, "No."

Incidentally, there are nearly as many men as women who think off-color jokes are objectionable in the workplace. That goes for foul language, too. Recently, one of our temporaries asked to be removed from his assignment because of the boss's foul mouth.

Sexual Innuendoes from Boss

Dear Jean,

I'm a 28-year-old SBM (single black male). One of my bosses, a woman, is constantly making sexual innuendoes. She's really attractive and I think she wants to date me. What do I do?

Reply:

When I read your question, I got the feeling that you may want to go out with her, too. If you're serious about your future with this company, avoid this romantic relationship at any cost. The overwhelming majority of boss/employee office romances end in disaster for the lower-ranking person. If you're planning to leave soon anyway, go for it!

I have a young male friend who is being sexually harassed by his boss, who is a female. When he is at his desk and no one is around, she will walk up behind him and massage his shoulders and his upper chest. Sometimes she bites him on the ear while whispering her graphic longings.

> **Sometimes the best thing to do is look them straight in the eye and say, "Stop that."**

At first he really enjoyed the attention, but after a while he was getting bored and fed up with her advances. The problem was, he let her behavior go on too long. Now she thinks that he is interested in her and has implied that to keep his job he has to "be a good boy" and comply with her desires.

Because he was not clear early on with his boundaries, he will be paying the price, most likely with his job. This doesn't have to happen to you. The first time the hair stands up on the back of your neck because of a boss's remark, clear the air right then. It becomes increasingly more difficult with each passing day and with each abuse.

I'm Married and He Keeps Coming On

Dear Jean,

A man who is best friend to my boss has made more than one pass at me while visiting our office. He knows I'm married, but he keeps coming on to me. Should I tell my boss that this guy he thinks is so great is nothing but a low-life lecher?

Reply:

I don't know what you mean when you say that he is making passes and that he is coming on to you. Is he making sexual comments? Is he telling you off-color jokes? Is he asking you to his bedroom to see his etchings? Is he massaging your neck and back?

If you answered "yes" to any of the above, here's the plan: The next time he approaches you in a way that you feel is unacceptable, tell him nicely and specifically what you think of his conduct.

This doesn't have to be complicated, and there is no need to stress out. Keep a cool head and calmly tell him that you are uncomfortable with certain behaviors, tell him exactly what those behaviors are, and that you would like for him to stop.

The goal here is to get the "offender" to stop his objectionable comments without having to go to your boss. Unless the guy is a total moron, he is likely to comply. If it happens after you have explained your disapproval, go directly to your boss.

Secret Love Notes

Dear Jean,

I work with a married woman who is sending me secret "love notes." She has been sending them for a couple of months now. They started out kind of innocent, but they have gotten worse lately. The last note was descriptive about how I could lie to my wife to get out of the house to see her. This is starting to get old.

I have no interest in talking to her, much less sneaking around to see her. I have told her two times that I feel uncomfortable about these notes. I've asked her to stop and they keep on coming. My wife thinks I should just ignore her. What do you think I should do?

Reply:

This is a form of harassment, and it is perhaps even more serious than you know. Someone who is as unhealthy as this woman is could severely damage your career. This is the type of person who 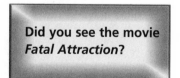 may become angered by your lack of response and accuse you of harassment. I don't want to get overly dramatic here, but did you see the movie Fatal Attraction?

Did you see the movie *Fatal Attraction*?

Don't open any more correspondence from her. Opening them makes you look interested. Go directly to your supervisor and show him or her the letters. The next thing for you to do is to consult a lawyer who works in the area of family law. Find out how to protect yourself. Please do this today!

Boss's Wife Has the Hots for Me

Dear Jean,

I work for an older man who is married to a much younger woman. Whenever she comes to the office, she stops by my desk on the way down the hall and chats with me. Here's the problem: She has begun to be more and more personal with her remarks, really coming on to me (I think). She is an attractive woman and I'm a single man. What do you think? Should I go for it?

Reply:

You think she is coming on to you? That's a pretty serious assumption. Have you considered the possibility that she is shy and is just finally getting to know you? There are a multitude of reasons for her friendliness. They range all the way from the possibility that she is in fact friendly to the possibility that her husband has asked her to warm up to you to evaluate your response. Maybe he wonders if he can trust you. In any case, if you fool around with this woman, you will most certainly be out of a job and maybe out of a future.

His Wife Wants Me to Lie

Dear Jean,

I have a boss who works out of town. His wife calls constantly wanting to check up on him and check on his expenses. Then she doesn't want me to tell him that she's been checking. I don't know whether to say something to him. I feel like I'm just stuck in the middle.

Reply:

It sounds like you are in fact stuck in the middle. There may or may not be a problem between your boss and his wife. Either way, you cannot be a conduit providing information to someone outside the office — even if it is your boss's wife. Expense reports are confidential company information.

You may already be in hot water. Have you thought about this: What if they are about to divorce and you are actually providing illegal information to her attorney? You have to stop this now.

Unless you think his wife is dangerous, get up your courage and go to your boss. Tell him about his wife's questions and her request that you not tell him about those questions. Tell him what information you have told her so far. Then ask him how he would like you to respond to her questions in the future.

Think hard about how you feel about the responses he would like you to give. If anything makes you uncomfortable, tell him so. You do not have to lie for him, and you cannot be an information leak. Be very careful with this.

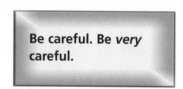

Be careful. Be *very* careful.

Not every office dating situation is bad. If people have something positive to look forward to at work, whether it is a good friend or a possible spouse, their attitude at work can improve immensely. Managers cannot keep their employees from being interested in each other, and it is pointless to try. They can't pass laws or make policies to stop people from falling in love. It will happen anyway. As Dennis Powers says in his book *The Office Romance,* "Owners, managers, and shareholders alike have concluded that it's none of the organization's business, and, given the very nature of people, that they would become involved anyway."

If you are careful not to let your dating situation interfere with your work, you could pass this minefield unscathed. Also, if you plan to date someone in your office, date someone who is on a comparable level in the corporate hierarchy. Both of you will be less likely to get burned.

Sexual issues are never simple and are always central. The fact that they come up in the office, where people spend nearly half their waking hours each week, only intensifies the problem. The most important advice I can give you when it comes to sex and romance in the office is this: Be careful. Be *very* careful.

Points to Remember

☐ Sex, gossip, and spying are fun, but risky.

☐ Intracompany dating can be dangerous.

☐ When people around you are gossiping, stay quiet or leave the room.

☐ When dating co-workers, consider the best and worst possible outcomes.

☐ Unless a situation directly affects your ability to make a living, it's none of your business.

☐ The overwhelming majority of boss/employee dating relationships end in disaster for the lower-ranking person.

☐ If someone makes an unwelcome sexual advance, look him/her in the eye and say, "Stop that!"

☐ Lying for your boss will put you in the crossfire.

Rudeness, Rules, and Rituals

3

Many people say that training in manners is obsolete, unimportant, and trivial. Think how much nicer the workplace would be if everyone demonstrated courtesy. The whole idea of courtesy at work is to make the workplace a nicer experience.

Some years ago, I had an assistant who was bright, efficient, and lightning fast. Two people reported to her, and a lot of informal written correspondence passed among her and her staff members. During her first few weeks, I sensed a slight resistance from her staff.

At about that same time, I noticed that in her writing she never used the words please or thank you. When I asked her about this, she told me that she thought please and thank you were implied and not necessary to include in informal correspondence. She also said that it takes time out of her busy day to remember to write them out every time.

My assistant was willing to change, and as a result of this slight and important modification in her writing and behavior style, she was able to get 100 percent cooperation from our administrative team.

Are we really too busy in the workplace to be polite? How do you feel when your boss is impolite to you?

The Rules

Among the many "rules" in society, two main rules come to mind, the Golden Rule and the Platinum Rule. The Golden Rule is: "Do unto others as you would have them do unto you." When that one fails, use the other one, the Platinum Rule. The Platinum Rule is: "Do unto others as they want to be done unto."

The Platinum Rule may be more important than the Golden Rule because people have certain expectations about how they want to be treated. The problem is, they don't tell us those expectations. We have to figure them out.

For instance, I have a colleague who gives off a confident air. She is very direct and powerful. She is smart, competent, and influential in the community. She is quick to make decisions and voice her opinions. She appears to have it all together. However, while she projects this self-assured, direct image, she is secretly wanting you to be extra careful when you choose your words, especially if you have anything unpleasant to say to her. In other words, it appears as though she can "dish it out but can't take it." She is surprisingly sensitive and rarely gets compliments or empathetic concern from her friends or family. The vibes she gives off are not the ones she wants back.

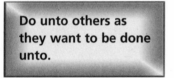

Do unto others as they want to be done unto.

On the other hand, there are mild-mannered people who are caring and compassionate and want no empathy at all. They don't want you to make a fuss over them and are even embarrassed when you give them a compliment. Learning how to "do unto others" is work, but the rewards are immediate and lasting.

Rituals are important, too. To avoid rudeness, you have to follow the rules and buy into the rituals. Unfortunately, rules and rituals aren't generally posted conveniently so you can refer to them when you need to. You have to learn them as you go. Most of us learn these things the hard way. We make a mistake that causes us some kind of grief, so we become willing to listen. Then we adjust our behavior to fit the culture.

Culture varies from country to country as well as from company to company. All companies have cultures, and the expectations of behavior are usually consistent with that culture.

Current studies show that most people spend more time with their co-workers than they do with friends and family. Because of this, our co-workers can become, to some extent, part of our circle of friends. Often, we are so close to our co-workers that they seem like family. This attachment is thrown into flux when a co-worker or a co-worker's family member becomes seriously ill or dies. Because they are "those people we work with," what steps are acceptable? What can we do in these situations?

Most people are unclear about what is required, what is allowed, and what will be most helpful if someone connected with our office becomes sick or dies. We also are not sure how much we are allowed to grieve. Is it OK to show our worry and grief, even though this person is merely a co-worker? For example, what if your boss becomes ill?

Boss in Hospital

Dear Jean,

My boss was hospitalized recently. Should I go visit?

Reply:

That depends. I use the Platinum Rule in this situation: "Do unto others as they want to be done unto." That means just because you would like visitors at your hospital bed does not mean your boss wants visitors. Many people aren't up to entertaining in their bedclothes. Check with a family member and ask if your boss is receiving nonfamily visitors. Usually, a steady stream of clever cards and get-well wishes is enough. Flowers couldn't hurt.

Some people really want to be visited when they are in the hospital.

Dear Jean,

Your question about the boss who was hospitalized really touched a chord for me. I was in the hospital recently and no one from my work visited me at all. I live alone and don't have much family in the area, so I really felt all alone. I would have appreciated a visit. As a result of the aloof treatment of my boss and co-workers, I have built up a few resentments. I just wanted to say to your readers, don't just assume that someone doesn't want to be visited when sick. Sometimes that's when a person really needs to see a friendly face that is not attached to a syringe.

Staff Member's Child Has Cancer

Dear Jean,

One of my key employees informed me that her child has cancer. Our company department is rather small and this has hit all of us really hard. I'm sure this illness will require my staff member to be off work a lot, and when she is here, I doubt if she can concentrate. I need to meet with her next week. What shall I tell her?

Reply:

By the time you talk with her, some of the initial shock will be over. Please remember that she is dealing with a gripping fear. How you handle this event will determine your relationship for years to come. Listen carefully to what she has to say. Let her "talk it out" with you. After expressing your genuine concern, tell her what you can and cannot do as a manager. Be really specific about the guidelines your company has set up to deal with a crisis like this. You may be going down a very long road, and your employee needs to feel secure in knowing exactly what is expected of her.

As far as being able to concentrate on her job, there is no way to know how a person will react under extreme stress. She may do fine. Cross that bridge when you come to it.

If a co-worker's child becomes ill, it can seriously disrupt not only that employee's work but also morale throughout the office.

Julie Kinnard had worked for Dow Services for 15 years. She was the word-processing supervisor. Everyone liked her.

Julie's daughter, Kerry, was only five when she was diagnosed with cancer. She was a spunky girl who loved to sing. She was a born entertainer. Everywhere she went, she gathered an audience. The day Julie learned of her daughter's illness was a rough day for the whole department.

It was so hard for everyone to know what to say or to do. People were crying, and very little work was getting done. After a while, the department got back to business as usual, but each time there was a change in Kerry's health or a new round of chemotherapy, a cloud seemed to hang over our department.

When Kerry died, Julie's fellow employees seemed to put themselves in her shoes. Most of the other employees had children and were saddened to the bone to hear the news.

When Someone Dies

All of us at one time have heard the grim announcement of a friend, a friend's family member, or a colleague being diagnosed with a grave illness or, worse yet, dying.

Nothing in the workplace requires more purposeful care than dealing with death and illness. Every one of us, from time to time, will feel it necessary to write a sympathy card or make a difficult call to someone we care about.

Should We Notify Our Clients?

Dear Jean,

My employer lost his wife this year. We have a large number of clients, and not all of them know about his loss. He doesn't want to notify them. He wants to just wait for them to walk in and then tell them. I think this is very cruel to our clients. It puts them in an awkward position. He's done this to a couple of clients and they came out totally shocked because she had been gone for months and they didn't even know about it. I don't know how to approach him about it, but I'd like to try to get him to do it differently, to notify them in some way. What should I do?

Reply:

I do agree with you and your feelings on this, but he's still in grief. His wishes about who he tells are really his business. Maybe you can convince him in a caring way to notify your customers or to let you notify them, but the bottom line is he is the boss and he is in grief. His wishes are what have to stand.

The above situation is another in which the Platinum Rule applies and the Golden Rule doesn't. The writer is coming from a position that he/she feels very strongly about, but the fact remains, it is the boss's business.

Flowers for Funerals

Dear Jean,

One of my employees had a death in his family. I sent flowers to the funeral home. Are flowers always appropriate? Would a donation to a charity be better?

Reply:

That depends. Guidelines for flowers differ depending on religion and culture. At Protestant funerals, flowers are appropriate unless the family expresses a preference for a contribution to a favorite not-for-profit organization.

At Catholic funerals, flowers can be sent to the funeral home, whose employees will take them to the gravesite because flowers are restricted on the main altar. You may want to mail or deliver a mass card. A mass card may be obtained at any parish from any priest. A donation of $5 to $25 is appropriate. On the mass card, the priest will record who will say the mass as well as the time and date. This is published in a weekly bulletin.

At Jewish funerals, flowers are not appropriate. You can, however, send a basket of fruit to the family or make a donation to a charitable organization. It would be thoughtful to find out if there is a preference in the choice of charity.

In the Muslim religion, sending flowers to the home of the bereaved family after a call of condolence will be appreciated because some mosques do not allow flowers. A donation to the deceased person's favorite charity or a gift of food to the family is a nice gesture as well.

Sympathy Cards

Sympathy cards can be especially difficult. Many people avoid anything to do with death. Because they don't have experience with the delicacy of the situation, they are afraid of saying the wrong thing. If you knew the deceased person even a little, it is always nice to jot down in the card something about the person such as a happy memory or a generosity the person was known for.

In the letter below, you will see some words and phrases that can help you express your feelings.

What to Write in a Sympathy Card

Dear Jean,

Recently, the spouse of a co-worker died in a car accident. We were all shocked. I sent a nice card with a comforting printed statement. My wife told me that I should have written something personal in the card. I have the hardest time thinking of something to write. Can you help?

Reply:

A printed card is not in bad taste; however, most people agree that a paragraph or two is a bit more personal. Writing nothing on your card is better than writing the wrong thing.

Please avoid phrases such as, "I know how you feel." You can't possibly know exactly how they feel. Other examples of what not to say include: "He's better off now." "There is no pain where she is going." "Maybe it's a blessing that she went so fast." "He had a good, long life." "At least you had her for six good years."

And worse yet: "It's God's will." "We never really know God's plan." "God doesn't make a mistake." "There are no accidents in God's world." "God must have special plans for you to send you this great burden." "God never sends us more than we can handle." You may believe this 100 percent, but these words are not especially comforting.

Even if you are of the same faith as the bereaved, please subdue the urge to offer abstract·explanations of God's intentions. I'm not suggesting that you refrain from sending prayers and readings, because this may be most comforting. What I am saying is that unless you know the bereaved extremely well, it is best to use more concrete language in your letter.

Hear are some examples: "I am shocked and saddened to hear of your loss." "I feel fortunate to have known her." "We are all grieved to hear of your loss." "I want you to know how much I grieve for you." "What a shock it was to hear of the loss of your mother." "She will be greatly missed." "Please accept my deep-

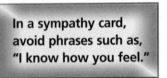

In a sympathy card, avoid phrases such as, "I know how you feel."

est sympathy." "We were so upset to hear about your accident." "I am so sorry to hear of your tragic news." "I could hardly believe the shocking news." "I will always remember him for...." or any combination of these sentences.

Sympathy letters should be handwritten. A subtle foldover card, your personal stationery, or a commercial card are all acceptable.

When is a sympathy card needed? It is not necessary that you know the person who has died to send a sympathy card. There are some instances that seem borderline, but when you are in doubt, do something.

Sympathy Card for a Miscarriage

Dear Jean,

One of my colleagues had a late and sudden miscarriage. I felt a little odd about sending a sympathy card since the baby had not been born. Did I do the right thing?

Reply:

Yes, you did. I am told that the death of an unborn baby is shattering. You were very thoughtful. Your sensitivity is refreshing. Your card may be one of the only formal acknowledgments of the tragedy. Thank you for your question.

Here is a note from someone who had been in the situation herself:

Dear Jean,

You are right about sending a card for a miscarriage. I had a miscarriage recently. A few people sent cards, even flowers. I didn't know how to deal with it myself and it helped to see acknowledgment of my loss in the cards. It somehow made it more acceptable. I am ashamed to say, though, that I did not return their thoughtfulness with a thank-you note. If I am ever in a similar situation, I hope that I handle it better.

Sympathy Card for a Pet

Dear Jean,

My employer has been divorced for several years and up until last week, he had a German shepherd roommate named Pal. Pal died last Tuesday and my boss is devastated. My inclination is to send my boss a sympathy card. It seems like a really sappy thing to do, but I would be in mourning if something happened to my cat. If you were me, would you send a sympathy card?

Reply:

A pet sympathy card or a handwritten note would be fine. Many people are as attached to their pets as they are to their family members — in some cases, more so. If you are like me, this is a very difficult type of note to write.

It's a nice gesture to write a few sentences as you would if you were sending a traditional sympathy card. Say something like this: "I was sorry to hear that Pal died. I know he was a good friend and an important part of your life. Just want you to know that I am thinking about you and your loss." If you had any dealings with Pal, you saw him fetch a ball, etc., you might want to tell about it in a sentence or two.

Your note may be the only acknowledgment of loss he receives. I'll bet he will admire you for your gesture.

Unresponsive Colleagues

Dear Jean,

Recently, my husband's mother died. I am in a new marriage. This has been very upsetting to my life. Not one of my friends or business associates sent me a sympathy card, acknowledgment, or note of support. Isn't this bad manners?

Reply:

I'm sorry to hear that your friends didn't acknowledge your grief.

After checking several sources of accepted etiquette, I have not been able to find anything written on sympathy cards regarding in-laws. I can't say

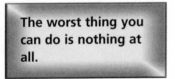

The worst thing you can do is nothing at all.

categorically that their neglect is bad manners. But I can say that your point is a good one. Let's start a new ritual.

As for your feelings, you may want to tell your friends how much their support was needed. Maybe they'll be more responsive in the future. There are a good many women who would find some gratification in being in your shoes.

Those are the women who think the only good mother-in-law is an absent mother-in-law. It is also quite possible that they weren't aware of her death.

If, after careful examination, you still feel you were ripped off emotionally, add some new people to your list of friends.

Returning to the Office

Once a co-worker has gone to the hospital and has been out of the office for awhile for one reason or another, it becomes increasingly hard for that person to return to the office. As a co-worker, you don't want to ignore the situation, but you also feel afraid of dwelling on it. It is necessary to find a happy medium.

Cancer Re-entry

Dear Jean,

I supervise a staff of 13 people. One of my staff members is returning from a long series of cancer treatments. I want his re-entry to be as smooth as possible. What can we do as a team to facilitate this? How should we act?

Reply:

It sounds like your co-worker almost lost his life, so please don't act as though nothing has happened. With a person returning to work from any serious illness, you can expect everyone to be somewhat uncomfortable. Some of his co-workers may withdraw completely. Believe it or not, some people still think cancer is catching.

Also, many people think if they ignore it, it will go away. These behaviors can be shattering to the person who is desperately wanting to get life back into a stable routine. It's also important to remember that everyone is different. Some people will want very little conversation regarding the illness; others will want more.

You as the manager can be really helpful by doing two things. One, ask your employee what kind of behavior on the part of the staff would make him feel comfortable. Two, call a meeting to discuss these concerns. Possibly you can get a person from the American Cancer Society or a counselor working in the cancer field to come to your office to give a short talk and answer all your questions.

Those of us in business don't talk enough about these challenges. Your letter may help hundreds of people. Thank you for taking the time to write.

Cancer is not a death sentence. Not too long ago, when you heard the word cancer you thought the word death. The cancer patient at work had a double challenge. Patients had to fight the illness and fight the attitudes of co-workers who would pull away from them. People don't cope well with death and serious illness. Attitudes are changing, however, and there are an impressive number of people who survive cancer.

Treatment Center Trauma

Dear Jean,

I am one of several midmanagers in a medium-sized manufacturing firm. We're a fairly close-knit bunch of people. Most of us know each other pretty well. One of my co-workers just returned from alcohol treatment. Should I act as if this never happened?

Reply:

It did happen, and I realize that this is really an uncomfortable situation. It's kind of like trying to ignore an elephant in your reception area; you can't do it for very long. Because alcoholism is considered an illness, you should treat this like any other serious illness.

You mentioned that you are a fairly close-knit bunch of people. My suggestion is to welcome your colleague back and bring him/her up to date on the business in general and that person's area in particular. If the employee wants to discuss treatment with you, by all means lend a willing ear. Otherwise, it may be good to say you're glad the employee's back, then stick with the things you have in common: work, children, hobbies, etc.

Recovering alcoholics have a big challenge ahead. To stay sober, they will have to change nearly everything about the life they knew. They will have to change their friends, and they will have to change their old ideas about how to live. To recover, they will have to embrace a new way of life which demands rigorous honesty. Alcoholism is a gravely serious illness which kills the majority of people it touches through accidents, heart disease, liver disease, cancer, or a host of other illnesses. Recovery also depends on a lot of meetings or outpatient classes.

If you are the manager of recovering alcoholics who have been in treatment, I'd like to make some suggestions. Anything you can do to allow some flex time will be helpful, especially in the beginning. Recovering alcoholics need a lot of support. They will most likely be involved in Alcoholics Anonymous or some type of outpatient program. 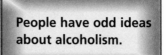 **People have odd ideas about alcoholism.** Some of these meetings might possibly be during the lunch hour. Give them the same consideration you would give to a person who needed physical therapy after an accident.

Make sure you do not discuss the alcoholic's illness or treatment with anyone. There are many inquiring minds out there, and this is none of their business. People have odd ideas about what alcoholism is. The word alcoholism conjures up pictures of skid-row bums — men — sitting on the street with a pint of cheap booze in their inside coat pockets.

The people I just described are the overwhelming minority. One person out of 10 is alcoholic, so out of every 10 people you know, one is an active alcoholic. One half of alcoholics are women. Many are teenagers. For more information, visit www.alcoholics-anonymous.org.

Return from Mental Hospital

Dear Jean,

My co-worker has just returned from a self-imposed month in the state mental hospital. My problem: What shall I say or do? How should I act around this crazy man?

Reply:

You will want to treat this person as you would treat any person returning from a stay in the hospital because of a serious illness. First, welcome your co-worker back. Second, make sure he is briefed on all projects of importance. Hopefully your boss will be on the ball and make sure your fellow co-worker has a project or two and a deadline.

As far as what you say or don't say, avoid talking about his treatment. If he brings up the subject, of course you will listen. Don't ignore the conversation, but don't probe.

By the way, the person who ignores his psychological problems and refuses to seek help is the one who is "crazy." Your co-worker did the smart thing. He got help when he needed it.

Manners: The Many Pitfalls

Manners are the grease on the gears of the office. If our manners are good, everything runs smoothly. Unfortunately, there are many types of manners and many pitfalls. I can't talk about every pitfall out there. That is a whole book in itself. If you want all the details, I suggest you buy an etiquette book. Here are some examples, however, of the depth and breadth of questions about manners.

Postcards Are Not Rude

Dear Jean,

I find postcards easy to write, send, and receive. Another salesperson who works with me says I'm being rude to contact my clients with "cheap postcards." He uses a first-class letter. Tell me, Jean, do you think I'm being rude?

Reply:

Gee, I hope not. I send about 10 postcards a week.

Your question piqued my curiosity, so I went to my etiquette books. So far, I have not seen anything written on the subject.

This, of course, is a matter of preference and there is no right or wrong answer, but I do know that we all love to receive personal mail. Isn't it true that when we open our mail, the first thing we do is look for something addressed by hand?

Unless a customer complains, keep up the good work!

Here is someone who disagreed:

Dear Jean,

I disagree. I think postcards are impersonal and show that the sender is lazy. Whenever I get a postcard, I wonder how many people read it on the way to my desk. When I get one from a salesperson, I figure they are just trying to get extra mileage out of the other people who read it. Postcards are so small that the sender doesn't have to write much or think much about the note. If they have something to say to me, they ought to send me a real letter.

Reply:

I am sorry you feel that way about postcards. I still feel they are a fun way to send a short note to a friend or a client. Someone who really was lazy wouldn't send a note in the first place. Maybe you are expecting too much from those around you.

Closed Meetings

Dear Jean,

My partners and I have a lot of meetings behind closed doors. Sometimes I'm in these meetings, sometimes I'm not. I'm curious to hear if there are any guidelines to interruptions regarding this kind of meeting.

Reply:

Meetings behind closed doors generally happen for a reason. They are either confidential or they require great concentration on the subject that's being discussed. In any case, these meetings shouldn't be interrupted unless the nature of the message is vitally important, as in the case of a client or family emergency. At that time, it is permissible to knock. Wait for an answer and hand a note to the person involved.

Another rule of thumb is to ask yourself, "Can this emergency wait one hour for a response?" If it can, avoid interrupting the meeting. If you're just curious and would like to manufacture a reason to enter the meeting room merely to see what's going on, you're on the wrong track.

Introductions

Dear Jean,

I'm the executive director of a small, not-for-profit concern. It seems like every day I'm in a position where I have to introduce people to each other. I know there are rules for proper business introductions. What are they?

Reply:

Business introductions are slightly different from those in social situations. The lower-ranking person is introduced to the higher-ranking person. It

A commoner is introduced to a queen.

will sound something like this: "Mark, may I introduce you to our vice president, Julie Fallone? Julie, this is Mark Matrol. He is our newest sales rep." Or "I'd like to introduce our vice president, Julie Fal-

lone. Julie, this is Mark Matrol, our newest sales rep."

As for social introductions, here are those guidelines:

    1. A man is introduced to a woman.

    2. A young person is introduced to an elder.

    3. A less important person is introduced to a more important person.

    4. A commoner is introduced to a queen.

Name Tags

Dear Jean,

I attend many conventions, conferences, and trade shows where name tags are required. I have noticed these name tags being worn by some on their right side and by others on the left. Which is correct?

Reply:

There is not a right or wrong answer to your question. Most people agree, however, that the name tags should be worn on the right side. That way when people are shaking hands with you they can see your name faster as you shake hands. If they can't remember your name, they look a little less conspicuous glancing at your right shoulder than at your left.

Additionally, if you prepare your own name tag, write your name very large. Anything you can do to help people remember your name will aid you in the future. If you are in the type of position where it's imperative that people remember who you are, be sure to get their cards. When you return to your office, send them short notes. It's a nice touch.

Tipping

One area that seems to be a particular bone of contention is tipping — how much, when, where, and who should do it.

Who Tips What?

Dear Jean,

Several of my colleagues and I are attending a conference together with our boss. The trip is paid for by the company. Should we expect our boss to handle taxi, tips, and so forth?

Reply:

You didn't mention in your question whether you have an expense account. If you do, you will pay, then submit the expenses for reimbursement. If you're not on an expense account, you should take some extra cash on your trip. When your boss accompanies you in taxis, your boss will pay. Otherwise, luggage, cabs, concierge, bellpersons, and waiters are all paid by you. There are recent books published on tipping. Check one out before you go.

To Tip or Not to Tip

Dear Jean,

I travel quite a lot on business and stay in medium-priced hotels. One of my colleagues tips the housekeeper $1 per day. She never sees this person. These hotels don't even have "turndown" service, no mints, no nothing. I think this is ridiculous. What do you think?

Reply:

If tipping is expected, you will probably see an empty envelope with your housekeeper's name on it. Generally speaking, these hotels charge in excess of $100 a day. Traditionally, most people don't tip in the United States unless they are staying at a posh resort (in Europe, this differs slightly). The going rate for that would be about $3 to $5 a day. A tip is appropriate, however, when you receive unusually good service, whether at a Motel 6 or a Ritz-Carlton. It's my bet that the housekeepers accept your friend's $1 a day with tears of gratitude. They did, after all, scrub that toilet bowl for her, didn't they? Would you do it for what they are paid — even with $1 extra?

Remember what your mom always said: "It never hurts to be nice!" So quit picking on your good-hearted friend. Don't tip if you don't want to, but don't fault her for her niceness.

Tipping the Delivery Person

Dear Jean,

At my company, my department often works through the lunch hour and we order food in, such as pizza. Is it proper to tip the delivery person, and if so, how much?

Reply:

Yes, it's proper to tip the delivery person. Most people tell me that 10 percent is the going rate. You may want to sweeten the pot for bad weather.

Valet Tipping

Dear Jean,

Last month, I attended a benefit luncheon at a local country club. As I drove up, I noticed it had valet parking. I tipped $1 when the attendant took my car and $1 when he brought it back to me. How did I do?

Reply:

You did fine. Most people tip between $1 and $3 when the attendant delivers the car. If you receive unusually fast service or the weather conditions are grim, you may want to tip more. In many places, tips are split among the attendants at the end of the day to ensure that newer people get their share of tips. Incidentally, when you're on a tight schedule and need to leave in a hurry, a word to the attendant and a healthy tip up front will assure that your car is parked nearby.

Dinner Manners

The various dinners and seminars we attend are also a breeding ground for mishaps.

Do I Sip When They Toast Me?

Dear Jean,

I belong to a large trade association. Next month, I will be honored at our annual banquet. I understand that the president will present a toast. Do I also sip out of my glass?

Reply:

Congratulations on your achievement. You must be very excited.

No, you don't sip out of your glass, nor do you stand. Just sit there, smile, blush if you can, and feel good about yourself. You may be asked to stand briefly, just to let people know where you are.

I'll Keep the Napkin in My Lap

Dear Jean,

Recently, I was a guest of my company at an evening dinner program. There were eight people at our table. After the meal was completed and the speaker started, I noticed that several of the people at our table put their napkins on the table and several of them kept their napkins in their laps. Which is correct?

Reply:

At a restaurant, the proper thing to do is keep your napkin in your lap until you leave the restaurant. I've looked in all my books and have found nothing pertaining to napkins at after-dinner talks. Therefore, I'd like to submit the following napkin etiquette, according to Jean: After the lights are turned down and the speaker begins, either fold the napkin lightly and place it on the table, or leave it on your lap until you leave the meeting.

Food Faux Pas

And finally, food.

Which Fork?

Dear Jean,

My partner and I have a $10 bet going. It concerns table settings. When the entree and the salad are served at the same time, which fork is used? I say you can use your entree fork for both. What do you say?

Reply:

I say you can collect your $10.

Noncompliant Spaghetti

Dear Jean,

I was eating spaghetti the other day and it was not complying with my fork and spoon. What do I do?

Reply:

If you were out on a luncheon, this is a serious etiquette question. Traditional formal spaghetti etiquette calls for you to twirl your spaghetti on the side of your plate. Traditional casual spaghetti etiquette says you may twirl your pasta using a spoon instead of the side of your plate. Contemporary spaghetti etiquette is much more practical for the business diner. Peggy Post says in her book Emily Post's Etiquette 75th Anniversary *that it is OK to cut spaghetti with a fork. I enjoyed reading that, and I must admit that I've been cutting my pasta for years. I've saved many white shirts that way!*

Whether you are trying to use the right fork or just wanting to send a postcard, not stepping on others' toes can be tricky. Etiquette is both classic and influenced by changing times. When in doubt, though, I fall back on the old cliché: When in Rome, do as the Romans do.

Judith Martin says in her book *Miss Manners Rescues Civilization*: "It's once people are able to manage physical survival that manners become crucial. Then tradition is what gives society meaning and the rules by which we live are what make it work."

Points to Remember

☐ Say "please" and "thank-you."

☐ Treat others the way *they* want to be treated, not the way *you* want to treat *them*.

☐ In a sympathy card, avoid abstract explanations of God's intentions.

☐ The worst thing you can do when someone is grieving is nothing at all.

☐ If someone is hurting, avoid acting as if nothing has happened. Lend a willing ear.

☐ People don't care how much you know until they know how much you care.

☐ In relationship to the rules of etiquette, it is not important to always do the right thing. It *is* important to know the right thing to do.

Wired and Wireless

4

The telephone is only one of the ways we present an image through communications. Most people in the workplace also make use of faxes, pagers, and e-mail, to name a few. More and more ways to get our messages across are developing every day, and that makes handling those communications efficiently and politely an increasingly complex problem.

This chapter provides creative ways of handling the technology as well as the plain old communication problems we have every day at work.

Call Screening

"Well, it must be nice, those three-hour martini lunches your boss takes." I might never have heard this had I not walked in the door at the very time this remark was spoken. The visitor was my largest client, and I cared a great deal about what he thought of me and how I spent my working hours.

I had been attending an advisory meeting at our local community college. I certainly didn't want my client to think I was out partying, much less drinking and driving. The truth regarding my whereabouts would have been a perfect reason to explain my absence from my office.

Over the years, I have found that the truth about my whereabouts is both appropriate and interesting. "She's in a meeting," "He's gone for the day," "He left early," and "I don't know where she is" are all boring. Even worse, they leave callers with the impression that we are really not busy and just want to avoid talking to them. Not a good thing!

For those of us who have administrative support people answering our phones, it is vitally important to be aware of the messages we send. For those of us who occasionally answer the phone of a co-worker, the image we present is important as well.

In our office, phone training is rigorous. I'm a phone maniac. To help us train our staff on phone etiquette, we use the cassette program called *Phone Power*, by George Walther. *Phone Power* is distributed by Nightingale Conant at www.nightingale.com.

Screening Calls

Dear Jean,

I am one of those people who swore I would never have my calls screened. As a matter of fact, I thought my colleagues who asked their secretaries to do so were pompous and disrespectful.

Now I find myself so busy that I can't possibly answer every call I receive every day without working until 8:00 or 9:00 every evening. I regret this because I have always made it a priority to be accessible to anyone who called.

Many of the calls I receive can be handled by a member of our staff. Will you give me some ideas for polite call screening?

Reply:

It sounds as though you are at a point where you are legitimately too absorbed to answer every call or return every call.

Many people feel insulted by the bluntness of "Who's calling?" or "What is this call in reference to?" A more genteel way for your secretary to phrase this important question is "Will she know the reason you are calling?"

By asking this question, your trusted secretary will know if the call is urgent enough to disturb you, or if the request can be better handled by one of your staff. In any event, screening will free you to do more of the things that make a profit for your company.

In the service business, it doesn't matter how effective you are. It only matters how effective your client believes you are. Client or customer perception is reality.

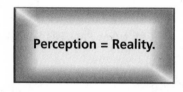

Perception = Reality.

How People Perceive Your Absence

Dear Jean,

I work 60 hours a week. Many of my meetings are at breakfast, lunch, and late in the afternoon. I try to keep the middle of the day open for client work. Recently, my banker asked me if I was ever in the office. I was horrified. My guess is she is calling at times when I'm out and she does not leave a message. I owe this bank a lot of money and I don't want to present the image that I work only when I feel like it. Any suggestions?

Reply:

Yes. How your banker perceives you is largely the result of how your office handles your calls. Possibly your assistant is saying things like, "She's not in yet," "She's not back from lunch yet," or "She left early and is not coming back."

There is a much better way to handle this. Make it clear to your assistant that you never want those phrases used. Replace them with, "She had a breakfast meeting and I expect her shortly," "She's meeting with a new client over lunch and will be back soon," "She's away from her office and will be returning after 5:00 P.M. Is there a number where you can be reached tonight, or would you prefer she call you in the morning?" Also have your assistant get a name and number and use the type of phone-message pads that produce a copy. That way you will know who has called and when, even if you no longer have the original message.

Screening calls is a tool which can make a busy executive's life much easier. However, screening can be taken too far. How do you feel when you are the person being screened?

Can't Get Past His Secretary

Dear Jean,

I need to talk to the boss about his secretary, but that same secretary screens all of his calls, so it is impossible to get through to talk to him. How can I get past her?

Reply:

Most bosses are extremely impatient when it comes to listening to complaints about the people they have chosen to be their right hand. I know I would be. Unless his secretary is doing something illegal, he will most likely not be interested in your complaints or opinions. If you insist on having his attention, you can send a registered letter which he has to sign for personally.

WARNING: This action could be hazardous to your career, so be sure to have a trusted mentor or colleague read your letter first. You will be glad you did.

There is a noisy minority of people thoroughly against call screening. They have very good reason to be against it. Call screening is for convenience. It should not require your assistant to lie for you. Neither is it a way for you to avoid talking to people you don't like or don't want to deal with. Call screening, if it is fair and effective, involves telling the truth to your callers and returning calls as soon as your schedule allows. It is the abusers that give call screening a bad name.

You Don't Have to Lie

Dear Jean,

One of my co-workers always wants me to lie when certain people call her on the phone. Is this right? Should I continue to lie?

Reply:

You don't have to lie for anyone, and if the "certain people" you spoke of in your question happen to be her supervisors, you could be in serious trouble. Before another day goes by, meet with her in private and explain your feelings. Avoid judging her behavior. Just say something such as, "When I mislead your callers, I feel uncomfortable, and I'm not willing to put myself in that position any longer." This will reduce your stress and make it clear to your co-worker that lying for her crosses your value system and you won't continue to do it.

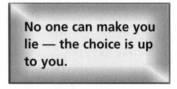

No one can make you lie — the choice is up to you.

Boss Won't Return His Calls

Dear Jean,

I'm having trouble with my boss. He is giving me a lot of things he should be doing that he doesn't want to do. He would rather be on the phone with his friends talking about sports and personal matters.

The problem is that a lot of people, mostly customers, are jumping on me because he won't call them back. I relay the messages to him, but he still won't call them. I get the idea that his callers think I'm lying. Do I tell him that he needs to be talking to these people, or should I go to his boss?

Reply:

I agree with you. I think that it is rude not to return calls, but what you and I think will not help you with this dilemma.

It's not a good idea to go to his boss. That will only add to your problems.

Just keep in mind that he is your boss, and he might have a strong negative reaction to your comments. Even if you stick to your feelings and refrain from passing judgment, your boss might still be offended. He might perceive your comments as "telling him how to run his business." Many employers are not receptive to employees making comments about the way they choose to do business. After all, you can't change him and there is nothing you can do to make him return his calls.

A helpful hint: You may want to change how you respond to the calls for your boss. Instead of saying, "I'll have him call you back" or "I'll tell him to call," say, "I'll give him your message."

You mentioned that your boss's callers are jumping on you when he does not return their calls. Be sure to put a time on all the messages you take so that when you get chastised, you can say, "I gave him the message at 3:25. I'll be happy to tell him you called again." This will not help you with your boss, but it will help you feel a little more honest.

So far as your boss having you do things that he doesn't want to do, that is called delegation. My hope is that you will experience delegation to some degree in every job you have. Delegation is what being a manager is all about. You aren't the only one who's being delegated to; your boss reports to someone who is delegating to him.

Personal Calls at Work

An enormous amount of work time is wasted each year as employees chat away with friends and family members while they are at work. There are many good reasons for employees to take personal calls. They may have a child in day care having problems. They may need to check that their latchkey children got home on time and are OK. A family member may be ill. When they are limited, personal phone calls are not a problem. When employees abuse their right to have personal phone calls at work, they are burning company dollars.

Personal Incoming Calls

Dear Jean,

There are seven people in my company. Five of my staff members have small children. My receptionist tells me that she takes 10 to 15 calls a day from the children and she's noticed that these calls are lengthy, sometimes as much as 10 minutes. I'm a single parent myself, so I understand the dilemma, but I have a profit to make here. How do I stop this?

Reply:

This is serious. Let's do some math. If your employees collectively receive 10 calls a day and spend 10 minutes on each call, that's 100 minutes a day of company time. When you add all of that up, it comes out to more than 430 hours a year of spent company time. Because time is money, these people are taking a lot of money out of the company coffers. You wouldn't let them write checks out of the company checkbook, so it makes sense to stop excessive personal phone calls of any kind.

Now, don't get me wrong. I don't think it's possible to stop all calls from children, and some of these calls can be vitally important. I'm suggesting that you talk with each individual privately and explain the math. Stay upbeat and state the problem clearly. Be sure to honor employees' feelings and listen carefully to their reasons for all these calls.

You mentioned that you are a single parent. Maybe you can share how you avoid receiving excessive calls from your children. Ask your employees what actions they will take to reduce these unnecessary calls. Set a specific follow-up date to review this problem.

There's another side to this coin:

Dear Jean,

I read your reply to the boss whose employees are getting too many personal calls. I have the opposite problem. My company has a "no personal phone calls" policy. We are not allowed to make any personal phone calls from the company and we are not allowed to receive calls either.

This has really become a problem for several employees, myself included. My husband travels sometimes, so he is not always able to handle all the problems with the kids, but I cannot be reached. There was one time when the school called with an emergency and couldn't reach either of us. Several times, my kids have missed the bus but were not able to reach anyone to get a ride home. I hate the idea of my kids being essentially abandoned from 8:00 to 5:00. What can I do?

My reply:

You probably cannot change the company policy, but there are some measures you could take. Maybe you could get a pager, the type that can alert you silently. Another idea is a wireless phone with voice mail. Then you will be able to check your voice mail while you are on a break. This is a win-win situation for you and for the company. You can stay in communication with your children, and they, or anyone who has your number, will be able to reach you. This allows you to receive messages from your children and not use company time to return the calls.

Here is another phone-call quandary. How many times have you been in a co-worker's or boss's office when she received a phone call? What should you do? Stay? Leave? Act interested in the paintings and listen in?

When They Get Calls

Dear Jean,

I'm a graphic artist for a large advertising firm. The work I do requires a lot of communication with my peers. Some days I have to consult with five or six people before starting my projects. I'm occasionally in a co-worker's office when he or she receives a phone call. Should I automatically excuse myself?

Reply:

Not necessarily. If the nature of the call sounds personal to you, you may want to go back to your own office. If not, you may want to wait it out. You can disengage and work on another project in your head.

Voice Mail

In the past, receptionists and secretaries took written messages. They took down the contact information and a few details on a little pink slip. As you returned from lunch or came out of a meeting, you would check your message box, pick up your stack of little pink slips, and start to return phone calls.

Many companies have automated their phone systems and added voice mail. This seems at first blush to be more efficient and more confidential. Often, though, we get so caught up in using the nifty new technology that it becomes less efficient than the old ways.

Voice-mail Overload

Dear Jean,

Every time I leave the office for a few hours, my staff loads up my voice mail. Often the questions are simple to answer one by one, but with so many of them, it usually takes me quite a while to go through them. If the question is complicated, I find myself writing it down. Do you know of any guidelines about how to leave and use voice-mail messages efficiently?

Reply:

In most cases, a long list of items should be communicated by the written word rather than by voice mail. Have your staff put their requests in writing. This will cut down on all but the most important communication. Voice mail is a luxury that many of us use for our own time management without regard for the time of the receiver. The written word is often the most efficient way, even if it is not the most technological way.

Another option is to consider changing your intraoffice messaging system to e-mail. That way, all the messages from your staff will already be written and easy to handle and answer.

Rambling Voice Mail

Dear Jean,

We use voice mail at our office, and I have a constant problem with the messages I get. Most of them are rambling, vague, pointless, and endless. I spend as much as an hour each day trying to decode voice-mail messages from the other vice presidents, my staff, and our clients.

Reply:

Sometimes we have to be especially clear about how we want to receive information. Design the message on your voice mail to give the caller an outline of what you want them to say. For instance, "Hello. I'm not at my desk right now. Please leave your name, number, time of day, and a message up to 30 seconds." Many people don't trust themselves when gauging their time, so you are likely to receive more concise messages of 15 to 20 seconds. At any rate, you won't be sitting through as many babbling voice mail messages.

Long Voice-mail Messages

Dear Jean,

My assistant leaves lengthy messages on my voice mail. She has a tendency to repeat everything twice. I call my voice mail frequently. Many times, I am calling from the car and I don't have time to listen to the same thing over and over. What do I do?

Reply:

Most of us have a tendency to treat voice-mail messages like conversations, and in conversations we often say things twice. It's a big challenge to remember that voice mail is used to transport pertinent information — period. Ask her to shorten her messages by half. Tell her that you have set a goal to do the same thing. Urge her to alert you if you are not practicing what you preach. Work on this goal together.

Whether you are leaving a voice-mail message or sending a fax, it is critical that you follow up with a confirmation. Read what can happen if you don't.

Always Confirm

Dear Jean,

I work at a small company where the owners and general managers work at a different branch and come to our branch about once a week. Every day that we need off, we are supposed to fax the request to them and let them know so they can make out the schedule there.

Well, about three months ago, I started faxing that I needed off for a week. I faxed this about twice a month for three months, and my manager said she never got it. Well, the day the schedule came out for that week, she told me that I had never faxed it because she had never received the fax. I got in trouble even though it wasn't my fault. I had faxed it to her. She had to rearrange everything because she didn't have enough employees to cover all the shifts. I got the time off anyway, but I was in a lot of trouble.

> **Always convirm vital messages, e-mails, and faxes.**

Reply:

Well, at least the right thing happened, but in a situation like that, you always want to have confirmation that your fax was received. Next time you fax something to your manager, you should call her a little while later to ask if she received the fax. Or you can put a note on your fax saying, "Please fax back to confirm that you received this fax." It's just following up.

This applies to voice mail, too. Don't leave an important message on voice mail and assume that the person you are trying to reach heard your message. Sometimes people don't regularly pick up their messages.

Recently, I drove to a nearby city to interview an accountant for a high-paying, high-profile position. It was an unusually demanding day and I was under more stress than usual. The drive was two hours. I arrived at the restaurant and I waited…and I waited. No candidate. As I started the drive home, I checked in with my voice mail. There it was — a message that she was not going to be able to keep our meeting time.

Speaker Phones

Have you ever noticed that you can tell immediately when the people you are calling are using speaker phones? Their words are clipped off at the first and last of every statement, you can hear echoes in the room, and their voices fade in and out as they move around rustling papers and things on their desks. What an irritation! Speaker phones are almost globally hated, but some busy executives still rely on them.

Get Me off the Speaker Phone!

Dear Jean,

I have a personal pet peeve — speaker phones. I can't stand to listen to someone who is receiving my call on a speaker phone. It usually cuts off most of the first word and some of the last word, and the echoes hurt my ears. What is a tactful way to ask someone not to use the speaker phone with me?

Reply:

When I want to be tactful, I might say, "Will you please pick up the receiver? I'm having trouble hearing you." When I am in an ornery mood, I might say, "Better pick up the receiver — I'm getting ready to say something you might consider confidential!"

Alternative to the Speaker Phone

Dear Jean,

I don't have time to sit around doing nothing while I am on the phone, so I often rely on the speaker phone to enable me to do two things at once. I've been told by some callers that they are annoyed by my use of the speaker phone, but I don't seem to have a choice. Do you have any suggestions?

Reply:

Yes. I, too, have that same problem. I am often put on hold and I have found that I can do a lot of work while I'm waiting. Here is how I solved my problem. I invested in a high-quality headset, the kind telephone operators wear. Shop around until you find a really good one. You might even call people who specialize in sound or radio to see if they can recommend a brand for you. It will be worth the money. A low-quality headset won't sound any better than your speaker phone, but a high-quality headset may sound even better than your handset.

Yes, you may look like you work the drive-thru at a fast-food restaurant, but you will save a fortune in chiropractor bills and massage therapy.

By the way, please avoid the temptation to do keyboard work while listening to the caller. Not only is it bad manners, it's not effective. People can't do two things well at the same time.

Wireless Phones

Wireless phones have revolutionized the office. Having a phone in my car allows me to keep in touch with my office and take care of all my voice mail while I am on the way to visit clients. With my car phone, I can use all that time that used to be wasted. Unfortunately, the use of wireless phones has brought its own set of problems.

The Phone Kept Ringing — at Lunch

Dear Jean,

Recently, I took one of my largest clients to lunch at a very nice restaurant. During our hour and a half together, her cellular phone rang three times. I realize she has a very important position, but I was really put off by these intrusions. What can I do about this in the future?

Reply:

There is nothing you can do about this in the future. For whatever reason, she feels she needs to be accessible to her office. Although you and I choose not to receive phone calls at the table, she does, and that's that. Granted, some people are not as considerate as they could be when it comes to pagers and wireless phones, but they were invented to make life easier for some of us, and they are here to stay. If she is one of your best clients, maybe you should plan an extra half hour for your lunch so she will have plenty of time to receive calls and talk business with you, too.

Other people are bothered by cell phones, too.

Dear Jean,

I just wanted to add my two cents in to the discussion on wireless phones ringing at lunch. I took my wife out to dinner at a romantic restaurant. As we sat there trying to keep a conversation going, at least three cell phones rang. Each ring was followed by a noisy conversation as the recipient of the call tried to be heard. It really put a damper on our romantic evening.

Here's my point. I know that cell phones are convenient — I have one myself. But the new etiquette with cell phones should be: RINGERS OFF IN PUBLIC PLACES. This means nice restaurants, auditoriums, libraries, meetings, conferences, seminars, theaters, and anywhere else where people are either trying to listen or where quietness is the rule. Thanks, Jean, for letting me get that off my chest.

Reply:

You've got a point there. Without much convincing, I might agree.

Dangerous Car Phones

Dear Jean,

I have heard that more and more car wrecks are being caused by the use of phones while driving. I am the manager for a large outside sales force, and often my salespeople check in with me on their car phones. Call me a worrier, but I know they are calling while driving to their next meeting, and it scares me. How can I keep my people checking in with me regularly, keep them safe, and not irritate them needlessly all at the same time?

Reply:

Invest in "hands-free" phone systems for your sales force. That way, they can call in when they want with less danger to themselves and others. The other alternative is to require them to call you while parked before or after their sales call. Now try that request with a prima donna salesperson!!

Long-winded Jerk

Dear Jean,

The other day, I was out in my car and I received a phone call from a long-winded jerk I never wanted to talk with in the first place. My new secretary had given him my phone number. I can't believe she gave this clown my cell phone number! Next, she'll probably have people calling me at my home. Shouldn't she automatically know not to give out my private numbers?

Reply:

No, she shouldn't automatically know how you want your calls handled. There is a likely chance that her previous boss had different preferences where the phone is concerned. I suggest you have an informal meeting to discuss the procedures you prefer. Explain exactly how you want her to respond to your callers.

While you are on the topic, it would be a good time to talk about other preferences, for instance, what kind of calls you consider important. I have also found it extremely helpful to provide the names of my close friends and family members.

What I am suggesting is a "win-win" situation. As a result of having this information, she will be more efficient in handling your callers, and you will not have to deal with this frustration again.

www.com

Although wireless phones are neat and all, the World Wide Web has brought the world together when it comes to communication. Its immense size and complication, though, are staggering. Have you ventured out on the Web yet? Are you ready?

Your Customers Will Tell You

Dear Jean,

I'm puzzled and even scared about all this talk about e-mail, surfing the Net, home page, and a dozen other electronic terms. My little company is getting along all right with a fax and a telephone. Do I need to jump onto the World Wide Web to do business these days? I hate the idea of doing that.

Reply:

I know just what you mean. I was puzzled about all those terms until I took the cyber plunge.

Back in 1989, I didn't have a fax. I didn't want a fax, and not having a fax didn't embarrass me one bit. As a matter of fact, every time one of my co-workers asked about buying a fax, I made it perfectly clear that I wasn't motivated to buy a toy for our entertainment.

One day, a client expressed frustration about our not having a fax. Then he bought me one! The rest is history. As far as getting a Web site, your customers will let you know when it's time. Ours did.

I've been on the Web for quite awhile, myself. I balked at first at making a presence for my company on the Web. It helped for me to start simple, with an easy e-mail system. As I got more used to it, I started to venture out on the Web doing research. What I learned there showed me that it would be vital for my company to be on the Web. It was that or be left behind in the dust of those who were ready to harness the magic of the Internet.

Now, my company has a dynamic Web site, www.jeankelley.com, and I do a considerable amount of communication using e-mail. Unfortunately, e-mail comes with its own set of annoyances. These next few letters are good examples.

E-mail and Bad Grammar

Dear Jean,

I receive more than 30 e-mails every day. I am constantly astounded by the lack of writing skills shown in this correspondence. I do not expect fine works of literature, but are spelling and basic good grammar too much to ask?

Reply:

There is e-mail and there is e-mail. If e-mail is used in the same manner that a formal letter is used, then I agree that the rules of grammar and spelling should apply. On the other hand, if e-mail is used to take the place of some phone communication, I don't mind the misspelled words and weird sentence structures.

Now, if you listen in on any spoken conversation, you know that good grammar is usually absent. Spelling isn't even a consideration. As we try to use e-mail in the same manner, grammar and spelling will suffer the same as in regular spoken conversation.

Here's a question: If e-mail was strictly required to always be perfect, would it take so long that we could no longer rely on it as an alternative to a phone call?

E-mail Madness

Dear Jean,

I am sick of all the idiots that send unnecessary e-mail. It is beyond me why some people have so much time on their hands at work. You wouldn't believe the jokes I get every day. These jokes are irritating to receive on my home computer. But at work, this is absurd.

And then there are the intracompany e-mails. Do you think I want to know that Jane Smith had a baby? Do I want to know that John Miller had surgery? Who is John Miller? I don't know these people. I must get 50 e-mails a day. As soon as I open my mailbox, I go into a rage. Do you have any suggestions for how to get less e-mail?

Reply:

Now there is an answer that could make me rich! With the exception of the rage, I can identify with the writer completely. I, too, have no idea why people have so much time on their hands at work. The time it takes to go through 50 e-mails to find the meaningful messages and then write a reply can be hours.

Hey! You out there...yes, you who are sending those meaningless e-mails, *please stop*. Some of us want to work.

People forward jokes to me every day. Almost all of them go into the trash. So far, I have seen only one forwarded joke that was meaningful. I've included it here.

Ever wonder why we are so overworked? For a couple of years I've been blaming it on lack of sleep, but I've been doing some research and have found the real reason.

The population of this country is 237 million.

104 million are retired. That leaves 133 million to do the work.

There are 85 million in school, which leaves 48 million to do the work.

Of this, there are 29 million employed by the federal government, leaving 19 million to do the work.

2.8 million are in the Armed Forces, which leaves 16.2 million to do the work.

Take from that the total of 14,800,000 people who work for state and city government and that leaves 1.4 million to do the work.

At any given time, there are 188,000 people in hospitals, leaving 1,212,000 to do the work.

Now there are 1,211,998 people in prison. That leaves just two people to do the work. You and me. And you're sitting there reading jokes.

Junk E-mail

Dear Jean,

It seems like every time I pick up my e-mail, there is some kind of advertising in my mailbox. My e-mail box is getting as junky as my regular mailbox.

I hate this intrusion. The very idea of paying "cyber dollars" to read junk mail burns me up. I hate it almost as much as having to sit through advertising at the movie theater. Is there anything I can do? What do you do?

Reply:

Unfortunately, there is not a whole lot you can do about this intrusion.

Sometimes the best reaction to this is not to react at all. Many of these messages include a statement asking you to e-mail them back to remove yourself from their list, but I have heard that this is not a good idea. When you send e-mail back to them, it tells them that they were sending to a correct address and that you took the time to read the message. They'll just send you more junk.

Personal E-mail at Work

Dear Jean,

My friend in Chicago is sending personal e-mail to me at work. The computer at work doesn't belong to me. She has her own computer and stays home all day. I don't have my own computer. What I do have is a demanding job and a demanding boss who wouldn't approve of my answering personal mail on the job. What do I do?

Reply:

You're right. Most bosses don't take kindly to people using company time and company equipment for personal use. So a good thing to do is explain to your boss that you have had some personal e-mail come through to the company mailbox. Be sure to apologize for having given out your company e-mail address.

Ask your boss how he feels about you receiving mail at work. Tell your boss that you are willing to talk to your friend and tell her that the company mailbox is off limits for personal mail.

Some bosses are willing to let you answer mail at lunch or after work, but unless your boss says it's OK to receive mail at work, tell your friend that the two of you will have to stick to snail mail until you have a computer at home.

Pornography in the Office

The vast, uncensored mass of the Internet has, in certain areas, linked itself to the lower instincts of many of us. Pornography on the Internet is a growing concern — and not just for schools. Internet access at work has allowed employees to bring pornography into the workplace with an ease that is frightening — especially to those who are concerned about the legal ramifications.

In the recent past, we wouldn't have secretly toted a *Playboy* or *Playgirl* magazine to work, much less an X-rated video. There wasn't a place for it, and no one would even have thought of it, much less actually have done it. Now all it takes it a click of a button, even an accidental one, and that type of material is displayed in full color on an employee's computer screen. What does this mean for those who are concerned about harassment?

Porn on the PC

Dear Jean,

A person I work with apparently surfs the Internet in his off time. He thinks it's funny to load porn onto my computer. He even puts these pictures so that they show on my screen in the morning. Now, I'm a normal guy who thinks that there is a place for this type of activity, but that place is not on my computer.

I have told this guy that I don't want to see these pictures, but he just laughs. I am afraid that my supervisor will see one before I can take it off and he will think that I put it there. How can I get this guy to stop?

> **If it's not work related, it doesn't belong on your office computer.**

Reply:

This is not a joke or some kind of male bonding technique. This is inap-

*propriate behavior in any office. Try one more time to get him to stop.
Don't tell him this in passing; have a sit-down meeting at his desk. Be specific about why you don't want to be part of his game. Document the conversation and keep it in a safe place in case you need it. If he keeps it up,
go to your boss.*

The scientific knowledge base is doubling every year. As a
result, our communications get more and more advanced, and
avoiding mistakes gets more difficult. It is so easy and fast to leave a
voice mail or send an e-mail. Unfortunately, if you make a mistake,
you can't get it back. It's already there. The recipient has already
received it.

I heard a story recently about a lady who was sending an e-
mail advertisement to thousands of possible customers. She spent a
lot of time developing it and finally determined that it was ready.
Right after she had sent it directly to all of these people's e-mail
boxes, she noticed a horrible mistake. In huge bold letters at the top
of the announcement, instead of saying "Public Auction" it said
"Pubic Auction." She lost her job.

Just remember when it comes to communications, whether it
is a phone call, a voice mail, a fax, or an e-mail, watch what you say
and how you say it. Just as if you were talking to the person directly,
you won't have a chance to take back what you said. Choose your
words wisely.

Points to Remember

☐ The truth is more interesting than a lie.

☐ Perception = Reality.

☐ No one can make you lie, the choice is up to you.

☐ Be aware of how long you talk when leaving a message on voice mail.

☐ When relying on technology to assist our communications, it is easy for things to fall through the cracks. Always call to confirm when you leave an important message on voice mail or e-mail.

☐ Before you automatically forward e-mail jokes, make sure the receiver wants them. If sending to a company e-mail address think four times before you send it. Is it clean? Does the person have time for this? Will their boss approve? Will your boss approve?

☐ Say no to porn on the office PC.

Parties, Lunches, and Dinners

5

Don't mix business with pleasure. I'll bet you've heard that before. Back in the '50s, that cliché meant something. There was a formality in those days that is no longer considered useful. Even as late as the early '70s, in some companies the boss was called Mr. or, in rare cases, Mrs. (and in even rarer cases, Ms.).

Now companies are becoming less and less formal. Not only are they relaxing their dress codes, they are also relaxing their company get-togethers, too. Rather than have the yearly formal "stuffed-shirt" dinner, they are encouraging staff members to get to know one another better in relaxed environments. Companies are sponsoring more charity events, athletic teams, and intercompany or even city-wide competitions in some areas. The focus is on fostering friendship and teamwork among co-workers.

In other words, not only are we spending our company time with our co-workers and bosses, we are also spending more of our "play" time with them. It is not always a good thing to spend so much time with the same people.

In today's companies, business and pleasure go together like green eggs and ham. They seem to fit together, but the eggs are still green. These company get-togethers are not without pitfalls. Occasionally, the social activities include situations that cross our personal, moral, or religious beliefs.

Christmas Party

Dear Jean,

Two years ago, my husband and I started a small manufacturing company. Although we are still pinching pennies, this is the first year we have had enough money to have a Christmas party. Our employees come from many different walks of life. Among those represented are various religions, races, and socioeconomic levels. It is difficult to be all things to all people, but we really want everyone to feel comfortable and we want to stay within a reasonable budget. Any suggestions?

Reply:

You mentioned cultural diversity in your company. The first thing to do is to find out if all your employees celebrate Christmas. If not, you may want to wait until after the holidays and have a New Year kickoff celebration. If you determine that all of your employees are enthusiastic about a Christmas get-together, I can think of a couple of low-cost options.

One is a covered-dish party. You supply the meats and beverages. Your employees bring the side dishes. Those who don't cook can provide chips, dips, and bread. If you prefer not to ask your employees to bring anything, a chili party at your home or business is a fun and inexpensive idea. You are out only the cost of chili, beverages, and extras. You may even have enough to buy each of them a small gift.

Should I Invite Her?

Dear Jean,

My secretary is a Jehovah's Witness. I am told she is not allowed by her religion to celebrate holidays or her birthday. Should I invite her to attend birthday parties of her co-workers?

Reply:

It is nice manners to give her the dignity of choice. Most likely, she will graciously decline. Because you don't fully understand her religious loyalties, ask. She will be delighted to tell you anything you want to know. Please don't assume. You may end up not inviting her to a baby shower she really wanted to attend.

I learned about the traditions of Jehovah's Witnesses firsthand from a most delightful person, our receptionist. It was I who almost didn't have a baby shower for her. Somehow I got the idea that Jehovah's Witnesses just said "no" to parties of any kind. Boy, was I wrong! A good rule of thumb is, "When in doubt, ask." Halloween parties are a definite "no" and anniversaries are a definite "yes."

No Compromise on Religious Traditions

Dear Jean,

Here comes another religious holiday (not my religion), and all the little kiddies will be hunting eggs at my boss's ranch. If I refuse to take my child to the big shindig, I'm a spoilsport. If I take her, I'm a hypocrite. Please help me, Jean. If you can come up with some compromise, I'll be eternally grateful.

Reply:

Based on the information you gave me, I don't see any need for a compromise. The party conflicts with your religious traditions, and that's that! You can explain that to your daughter in words she can understand. Remind her of all the fun activities that coincide with her own traditions as a way to soften her charge that you're a spoilsport.

I don't see any reason that you should be embarrassed about not taking your child to the party. Just send a nice handwritten note to your boss. Something like this would work well:

Dear Boss,

Thank you for your kind invitation to the Easter egg hunt at your ranch. Because the party conflicts with our family's religious beliefs, we must decline. We appreciate your generosity and thoughtfulness.

Sincerely,
Jane Jones

I Don't Celebrate Holidays

Dear Jean,

My religion does not celebrate Christmas, or any other holidays for that matter. Can I get into trouble at work for not putting up Christmas decorations, contributing to a gift for the boss, attending the Christmas party, etc.? It's not that everyone else celebrating bothers me; I just feel a bit strange taking part in this festival myself. Do you have any advice for me?

Reply:

There is no reason for you to participate in a holiday that is clearly against your value system. Nice manners on your part would be for you to tell your boss in advance that because of your religious convictions, you will not be participating in the festivities.

Over the last 10 years, we have had two individuals in our office who did not celebrate Christmas. In both cases, they told us up front that they would not be participating in the drawing of names, decorating the reception area, or attending our traditional holiday luncheon. Their wishes were honored by our company, and Christmas arrived and departed without a hitch.

One more thing — your boss may look with favor on your request. He or she would be thrilled to have someone attend the phones while everyone else is partying. Gather yourself some brownie points while observing your beliefs!

Here is a response I received:

Dear Jean,

It is true that employees are not really required to put up Christmas decorations and such, but there are exceptions. For instance, I am in a retail company. Our biggest moneymaker is, of course, the Christmas season. All employees are required to get into the spirit. For the week of Christmas, all employees are required to wear Santa hats as part of their uniforms and to wish every customer a merry Christmas. If an employee refuses, she probably wouldn't have her job much longer. Christmas is an important part of my business.

My reply:

Christmas is an important part of retail sales; however, it sounds as though you may be walking through a pit of snakes. One might reach up and bite you at any time. All it takes is one employee fired for this reason and you may have a powerful lawsuit on your hands. You cannot fire an employee on the basis of religious beliefs. If you do and the employee sues for discrimination, it could ruin more than your Christmas sales season!

An associate of mine ran into a similar challenge. She asked her public relations person, a Jewish woman, to dress up like a bunny to deliver Easter baskets to clients of the firm. The employee refused and was fired.

The company maintained that the Easter bunny had nothing to do with Christ and delivering Easter baskets was not particularly Christian. The fired employee argued that Easter was a Christian holiday and she would not be forced to celebrate. The fired employee won.

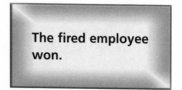

The fired employee won.

They Needle Me to Drink

Dear Jean,

I'm a lawyer and I work with a team of high-strung, deadline-oriented lawyers. Occasionally, after a long, intense day we go out together for a drink. Most of them drink quite a bit. I don't drink at all, but I enjoy being with the group. How can I keep them from needling me to drink?

Reply:

Just say, "I don't drink, thanks." The next time they needle you to drink, just say, "I don't drink." The next time — repeat it again....

Here is a response:

Dear Jean,

This is in reference to the person being needled to drink. I bet it sounds really easy to you to just say, "I don't drink, thanks." You've never been in that position, have you? I know I have! My wife really hates it when I drink, so I have made a deal with her that I won't drink with my friends anymore. I've promised to drink only with her. Now when I go out with the guys they razz me and call me henpecked, whipped, and other names. I've done OK (mostly) so far, but it is really hard. I just wanted to tell you that standing up to your friends isn't that easy.

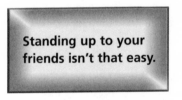

Standing up to your friends isn't that easy.

My reply:

I never said it was easy. I quit drinking many years ago and experienced the same problem. My friends said, "Why don't you have just one?" and "Come on — don't be a dud." It was especially hard my first few years, but it got easier with each response.

Client entertaining has always been an important part of my work. When I quit drinking, I was self-conscious — so self-conscious that I would get to the bar early, get a table, and make an arrangement with the waitress to give me ginger ale. If they didn't have ginger ale, I would order club soda with a splash of coke. Presto! I would have a drink that looked like scotch and soda. When the waitress made her rounds to take another order, I would just say, "I'll have the same."

Eventually I got up the courage to say, "I'll have soda with a twist" without any fear of reprisal. It sure made my life simpler.

Serving an Alcoholic a Drink

Dear Jean,

I have an employee who is a recovering alcoholic. Next month, my wife and I are having a party for my whole staff. Many of my staff members drink. I wonder if this will make this employee uncomfortable. When we ask our guests what they want to drink, what will we say to him? I would feel terrible if I were responsible for causing him to take a drink.

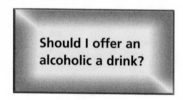

Should I offer an alcoholic a drink?

Reply:

You are not his mommy, and you are not responsible for his taking a drink. He is responsible for his own sobriety. As far as asking him what he prefers to drink, say something like, "What would you like to drink?" Avoid saying anything like, "Since you don't drink, maybe you'd like a Coke?" or worse yet, "Would you like a drink? Oops! I forgot." Even though your heart is in the right place, your comment comes off as too parental, maybe even insulting. He knows he's an alcoholic. He knows you know he's an alcoholic. You don't need to look after him. Just make sure that you have soft drinks available when he gives his order.

In pop psychology there is a term called rescuing. Rescuing is when you do something for someone that he can, and should, be doing for himself. In this case, when you make a decision for

Rescuing = Robbing

someone who is capable of making the decision for himself, you are rescuing.

Nurturing is helping a co-worker learn how to do a new task. Rescuing is doing that task for him. When you rescue a co-worker you rob him of the opportunity to learn on his own. Rescuing is when you do something for someone that he can and should be doing for himself. Give him the dignity to fail!

Office Entertaining at Home

What if the work-related party is supposed to be at your home? Entertaining at home can be fun. The thing to remember is that it is your home, so you and you alone set the guidelines.

Entertaining at Home

Dear Jean,

The longtime manager before me entertained the staff at several stated intervals during the year. Some of the employees have made remarks that make me think they are expecting things such as holiday dinners, cocktail parties, and birthday bashes at my house. How should I handle this? I like my privacy after working hours.

Reply:

Just because the manager before you had parties at his home doesn't mean you must. Have you asked your boss about this? My feeling is that if this was terribly important, it would have come up in your interview. But if your boss is the type of manager who promotes social events at his/her home, you may be expected to do so as well. If that is the case, you might get by with short "happy-hour" gatherings, say, from 5:30 to 7:00 P.M. If that is not the case, maybe you could arrange to have an occasional catered get-together at the office during the lunch hour. That may not appease the party animals, but chances are you'll sleep better knowing you haven't sent a busload of drunks out on the road after a six-hour party at your home.

A few years ago, there was a legal case in which a bartender did not stop a drunk from getting behind the wheel of the car. As I remember, the drunk had a car accident. A lawsuit was filed and the drunk sued the bar and the bartender for letting him leave the bar drunk. The drunk won. Go figure.

Be Direct with Smokers

Dear Jean,

Several people at our company smoke. I plan to have a big holiday party and I don't want these people smoking in our home. Should I make sure that nothing on a table looks like an ashtray and hope they get the hint?

Reply:

In a warm, diplomatic way, let them know that you have a smoke-free home. They'll know that if they attend your party they will have to abstain. Most smokers don't relish the idea of a whole evening without a fix, but some are now acclimated to the idea that the world no longer welcomes their vice. You may want to point out the back garden, the verandah, patio, or even the front steps as the best place to light up. They can understand taking a cigarette break from your party. They have to do that at nearly every office or place of business these days.

It's still true that we Americans are free to do as we please in our society so long as we don't harm ourselves or others or scare the horses. Research has proved that cigarette smoke is harmful for the smoker and for others in the smoker's vicinity. Right is on your side.

Business Concerns

There is a lot of racial and cultural diversity in the United States. It is my opinion that we need to be sensitive, whenever practical, to the traditions of all people. I also believe that we, as responsible, sensitive businesspeople, should make reasonable accommodation when we are asked to give an invocation. Here's an example:

Invocation Causes Interfaith Stress

Dear Jean,

I have been asked to give the invocation for a large luncheon meeting. Our guests at this meeting are people of various faiths. I don't want to offend anyone. Do you have any suggestions about how I should handle this sensitive situation?

Reply:

I understand your sensitivity. It is very hard to please all people with an invocation. The best attempts I have heard used the word Creator to describe the Ultimate Deity. Alcoholics Anonymous sometimes uses Higher Power. Either should offend no one.

Company parties can be a lot of fun. They serve as important business functions as well. Get-togethers out of the office are a way for employees to have a chance to get to know one another in different environments.

Many people are extremely serious at the office, but when they go to a party they really loosen up. The purpose of these outings is to create an environment where employees can drop their serious "work selves" and have fun.

This is not fun for everyone, however. Some employees look toward company parties with dread, even disgust.

Company Cookout

Dear Jean,

What I really hate is the annual "company cookout." Everyone overheats and overeats, and something disturbing always happens. Our boss expects us to show. Can I make excuses and stay home?

Reply:

I'm afraid not. Companies and families have a lot in common. Remember the last time you were invited to a big family reunion? Remember how you wanted to make excuses and stay home?

With the exception of situations that compromise our values, sometimes we have to suit up and show up. This may be one of those times. Buddy up with someone who won't overeat or overheat. Then the two of you can treat this as a spectator sport. Take a couple of lawn chairs. Get some popcorn. Enjoy the show.

Junior Is a Jerk

Dear Jean,

Every office has its comic, and our place of business is no exception. My co-worker (I'll call him "Junior") is a foul-mouthed jerk. He thinks he's cute, I'm sure. He is always chosen to be emcee at company functions such as the New Year kickoff party after the annual sales meeting. Even though everyone thinks he's a scream, I think he's an idiot. Can I stay away from the party?

Reply:

I can't make that decision for you, but I can run through the pros and cons of going to the company party.

Pros:

You might have fun.

You might get to know someone new and interesting.

You will affirm the esprit de corps of your company.

You might get to know your boss better.

You'll be able to lubricate your social skills.

Cons:

You despise the emcee.

What do you think?

> **You will not like every person you work with, but you will have to get along with them.**

There is most likely a jerk where you work (I hope it's not you). There will be jerks in every workplace. You are not going to like every person you work with, but you will have to get along with them. There's no getting around it.

I'm No Stick-in-the-Mud

Dear Jean,

I'm no stick-in-the-mud, but I've just heard some disturbing news about the company where I've just started to work.

It seems as though my new company has a holiday bash, and I do mean bash. The word is that this particular party is one of the wildest drinking occasions of the season. All of our suppliers are really looking forward to this event. The party starts at 4:00 in the afternoon and lasts until everyone leaves or just falls over.

I don't have a moral objection to drinking, but it does concern me that a lot of people will be leaving this party really smashed. I don't want any part of this scene, and I am expected to attend. What can I do?

Reply:

The information you received about your new company is hearsay. It does, however, sound rather convincing.

I know you feel that your attendance at this party is required, but no one can make you do something that is against your value system.

If you do decide to attend, please keep one thing in mind. You have no control over what other people do at a party. The only person you have control over is you. Drink soda, leave early, and offer a ride to anyone who will leave when you do.

I'm Shy at Social Gatherings

Dear Jean,

I have a real problem in social gatherings. I'm really outgoing until I get to a big party. I seem to do better at small gatherings. I'm extremely comfortable in a one-on-one situation. Is there anything I can do to relieve this nervousness in groups?

Reply:

I feel the same way in groups of people I don't know. Once in a while, I still end up in a corner talking to people I know rather than meeting new people. A party at my own office is a breeze. On my own territory, I know exactly what I want to gain from having the party.

The answer to your question lies in your reason for being at the party to begin with. Be clear with yourself. What is your goal? Are there people you want to meet? Is this purely networking for business, or are you networking for social reasons as well? Having a goal will help you walk into a room of mostly strangers.

My goal for a business party is usually quite simple — to make contact with two new people. After I've reached my goal, it's time to relax. It's important to me that the people I've met remember who I am and what I do, so when I return to my office, I send them a handwritten note with my business card.

I learned an interesting technique from a colleague at a National Speakers Association convention. He told me not to take business cards to a party. That was a little surprising to me. I always carried a purse full of them.

Here's what he said: "When someone at a party asks you for your card, say, 'Great! I'll mail you one. May I have your card?' That way, you get a chance to make a written impression as well as a visual impression."

Business Lunches

Business lunches are another essential part of our work lives. They are the ideal place for networking, strengthening business relationships, and even selling. It is easy to make mistakes, though. My first boss, who was grooming me for management, was always giving me good advice. It was important to her that I had the proper etiquette when I was representing her and her company in the community, and this was especially important when I started to entertain clients at lunch. Much of what I write about is what she taught me. The other stuff I had to learn the hard way.

By the time I was 23, I was entertaining clients for lunch. My boss told me: *"Always, always, always pick up the check when you take a client to lunch."* I replied, "What if the client is a man?" *"Always pick up the check,"* she repeated. Then I asked, "What if the client makes a lot more money than I do?" *"A lot of people make more money than you do,"* she pointed out. *"Pick up the check."* "What if they insist?" I asked. She did not budge. *"Pick up the check,"* she replied firmly.

One day early in my sales career, I asked a very important client to lunch. He was the president of an independent oil and gas production company. This was a man who was 20 years older than I, and he intimidated the heck out of me.

He was about 6 feet 4 inches tall and looked like a movie star. I was certainly not shy when it came to business, but I've got to let you in on a secret. I was shaking in my boots — not because this was a potentially huge client, but because he was so gorgeous.

Somehow, I managed to get through the lunch without dropping my napkin, spilling my tea, or misusing pronouns. The problem was that I had been drinking a lot of tea — a lot.

I excused myself from the table. I was in such a hurry to get to the ladies' room that I forgot all about *picking up the check.*

When I returned, the lunch was paid for. I knew I was in big trouble. Up to that point, I had been in trouble several times when it came to my expense account, but this was the only time I got chastised for not spending money.

Let Me Pick up the Check

Dear Jean,

I'm a female marketing executive for a worldwide insurance company. A couple of my male clients always insist on picking up the check at lunch. The lunch is always initiated by me, and I feel that because I invited them, I should pay. How can I manage to do this?

Reply:

This one is easy. Sometime during lunch, excuse yourself and find your waiter or waitress. Give him your credit card and explain what kind of a tip you want to leave. Then either have him bring the check to you to sign or arrange to sign at the front on the way out. Let your client know that when he invites you to lunch, he can pay. Once the relationship has developed over a period of months or years, make his day — let him pay now and then.

What I think is the most fun is to get to my favorite restaurant early and take a self-addressed, stamped envelope. I find the waiter or waitress who will be serving us, presign the check, and arrange for the tip. I then ask them if they will send me the receipt.

When my guest and I finish our meal, we just stand up and walk out. It always fascinates my guest and gives me a grin, too.

Talk Business before Lunch

Dear Jean,

Business lunches and dinners are great ways to build rapport. Everybody knows that. What everybody doesn't know is when to begin the business discussion and when to drag out the papers pertinent to the discussion. Can you help me?

Reply:

That's a good question. I, too, wonder if there is a definite right and wrong time when it comes to spreading papers out on the lunch or dinner table. I have checked several references and cannot find anything written in stone, so I'll respond by telling you how I handle this situation.

First, if it is possible, I avoid using lunch or dinner to make presentations of any kind. I schedule the important meetings in my office or theirs. There is not enough time or table space for a formal presentation.

At those times when sharing information over a meal is unavoidable, I engage in small talk until the food order is taken. A mentor once said, "Jean, people don't care how much you know until they know how much you care." So my small talk is geared to their interests, not mine.

As soon as the server walks away from the table, I briefly present my ideas. My intention is to finalize what I need to say before the salad arrives. If papers must be presented, then this is the moment to present them. If you can just hand the client a folder for him or her to read through at leisure, do that rather than spread the work across the table.

During lunch and dessert, I generally listen rather than talk. As I'm paying the check, I make any final comments and let them know when they can expect to hear from me again.

If you are like me, you know a lot of people. When you go to a busy restaurant, you may see a half a dozen people who come over to your table and say hello. Some restaurants are very loud, too. This becomes a big problem if you have more than a 10-

minute presentation. If that is the case, it is best to meet for coffee. I've found that some hotel cafes are excellent for this. Unless there is a big meeting at the hotel, you will have a quiet, nondistracting place to do business.

Order the Lobster

Dear Jean,

As the sales manager for a national company, I dine out a lot. Several of my clients are young, and I think their mothers told them to always order something inexpensive from the menu. How do I let them know that they can order something more expensive than a salad?

Reply:

Are you sure they want to order something more expensive than a salad? With such a health-conscious culture, it might be that they are more calorie conscious than cost conscious. However, if you really think they have a taste for the more expensive items, give them a hint. Say something like, "The lobster Newburg is great here" or "I'm ordering the filet mignon — what about you?"

My Boss Is Cheap

Dear Jean,

My boss is cheap. When he takes me to lunch, he insists on buying and he never leaves an appropriate tip. If the service is bad, he leaves a dollar or two. If the service is good, he leaves a dollar or two. I suppose the reason this bugs me is that I worked myself through college as a waiter.

Would it be bad taste to mention this to him?

Reply:

Enlightening him won't help you one bit and might even get you into real trouble. Executives aren't bad tippers because they don't know better. They are bad tippers because they choose to be.

Start worrying about something you have control over. Keep mum, chum, and work your way up to the head office. Then you can tip as lavishly as any ex-waiter might wish.

What if the Problem Isn't You?

Here you are, working hard to have good manners and make the right impression, but your lunch partner just doesn't get it. What do you do when the person you are taking to lunch has bad manners?

Expensive Lunch Cuts Commissions

Dear Jean,

I am a sales rep for an office supply company, and I have a limited expense account. My employer puts a limit on what we can spend at business lunches.

Here's my problem. One of my smaller customers always orders the most expensive item on the menu. He works at it, too. This really annoys me because anything over the limit gets subtracted from my next commission check.

I think this is rude. What do you think?

Reply:

Awww, forget rude — let's talk about what you have to gain. Experts agree that it's a lot less expensive to pay the additional few dollars than to go out and get a new customer. Grab your calculator. Let's say you take this customer to lunch every month and it costs you an additional $10.

At the end of a year, you are out an extra $120. How many hours did you put in to get this one account? If you are like most salespeople, you had to make quite a few calls to close this sale. I don't know about you, but if I could "buy" profitable small accounts instead of making cold calls, that's just what I'd do. Buy 'em — it's easier.

Now don't get me wrong. If you net less than $120 from this company a year, you would do well to give them to one of your competitors. But if you are getting a decent return on your investment — SMILE!

My Client Is a Drunk

Dear Jean,

I am in marketing for a CPA firm, and from time to time I am asked to do some entertaining at lunch. This is something I usually enjoy, but I have

one big problem. One of our major clients drinks a lot. Every time I take him to lunch, he drinks too much, makes a fool out of himself, and embarrasses me. My client is a drunk.

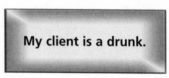

My client is a drunk.

I am not exaggerating. When the waiter takes our order, our client asks for three martinis. By the time lunch is over, he has had five drinks. He flirts with the food servers, tells lame, corny jokes, and bores me silly. What can I do about this dreadful situation?

Reply:

I'm glad I'm not the one having to take him to lunch. However, there is nothing you can do about the amount your client drinks. Likewise, there is nothing you can do about those corny jokes. The only thing you have control over is you.

I guess everyone in marketing has to take turns with this guy and this just happened to be your turn. Grin and bear it. He probably won't last long at the speed he's traveling.

(P.S.: At least you are the one driving.)

Client Loves Strip Clubs

Dear Jean,

I have a customer who wants to go to a "gentlemen's club" and get smashed every time he comes to town. He has so much as said that if I don't take him, he will find another supplier. I'm not totally backward, but I don't think strip bars and business are a very good mix. How about you?

Reply:

What I object to is a company forcing a sales rep or an executive to entertain clients in a gentleman's club. I'm not fond of drinking and driving, either. But this has gone on for years in certain industries and will go on for years to come.

So much for the problem; here's a solution. A friend of mine who is a sales manager for a large service company has a workable approach. He tells his sales people to take the customer to dinner, talk business, and then give the client the address to the gentleman's club.

Another friend of mine handles it a different way. She meets the client for dinner; talks business, goes with them to the gentlemen's club, and leaves after one drink. Maybe one of these solutions will work for you.

As you can see, there are arguments on both sides of the fence.

Dear Jean,

My company has been entertaining at gentlemen's bars for 30 years. That's the way we do business, and our clients like it just fine. You just don't get it, do you?

And there is this:

Dear Jean,

Yes!!! Thank you, Jean. I am a 35-year-old woman who sells construction supplies. I have been at my job, and at the same company, for 10 years. I have observed the other salespeople (who are men) take their customers to the strip bars, and I am at a distinct disadvantage. I'm glad you don't approve. There's too much cheesy behavior in the workplace anyway.

Earlier in this chapter, I mentioned my first boss. When I was a spunky 21-year-old, I was invited to a party at her home. All our big clients were at the party. I was expected to make a nice impression and to represent my department well. I *did* make an impression. I got drunk and demonstrated my knowledge of four-letter words.

The next Monday morning, my boss was walking around the company with a hat. There were coins in the bottom of the hat. She walked into my office and asked me if I wanted to contribute. I said, "To what?" She said, "We'd like to send you to charm school. We are hoping they can teach you to say *fantastic* instead of &%#$!"

I didn't end up going to charm school, but I did eventually learn my lesson. Company get-togethers, client meetings, and office parties may be held out of the office, but that doesn't mean you can completely let go of your "company" manners. The boss is still watching.

Points to Remember

 Be aware that others in your company may have religious beliefs that are different from your own.

 There is no need to compromise on your religious traditions or beliefs.

 Asking someone to comply with your traditions can get you sued.

☐ Nurturing is helping a co-worker do a new task. Rescuing is doing the task for him/her. Nurturing is OK, rescuing is not.

☐ Be diplomatic as well as direct.

☐ It is not important that you like your co-workers. It is important that you get along with them.

☐ The only person you have control over is you.

Giving and Receiving

6

Gifts are symbols. If you don't believe it, talk to a woman who didn't receive a card or gift from her sweetheart for Valentine's Day. In this case, the absence of a gift equates to the absence of love. Like it or not, the gifts you give at home or at work say a great deal about you. Don't believe for a minute that it is the thought that counts. It's the gift that counts.

All of us over 25 years of age have been guilty of giving a gift that the receiver did not especially want and didn't enjoy (surely you've received a gift you didn't like). The way we made that mistake was to give a gift that we ourselves would like without giving much thought to what the recipient would like. In matters of ethics, the Golden Rule is a good way to live. When giving gifts, forget the Golden Rule. You might end up with a mess on your hands. Use the Platinum Rule: "Do unto others as they want to be done unto."

I remember the shock and dismay when a young friend of mine received luggage from his wife for his birthday. They were newlyweds and he had a job in which he had to travel quite a bit. To him, the gift of luggage was a symbol. He thought it meant that she wanted him on the road more. That's not at all what she wanted. She was thinking about

> **It's not the thought that counts, it's the gift that counts.**

what she would like. She thought that if she was on the road a lot, she would like nice, attractive luggage with wheels on it. He didn't. He was happy with his old, beat-up, hard-sided Samsonite.

Another example of a gift as a symbol is a clock I received from my first mentor and boss. The clock was gold, round, and about four inches in diameter. It sat daintily on four little twisted and curved gold feet. It was delicately detailed and looked as though it belonged on a Victorian vanity. The card read, "Be aware of every precious moment of your life." The sentiment sounded innocent and gracious. You see, my boss was trying to teach me better time-management skills. The unspoken symbol of the clock was an elegant way to get her point across.

I'm not suggesting that every time you receive a gift, you try to analyze the giver's reason for giving. I am suggesting that you give thought to the gifts you give in the workplace.

Equality in Gift Giving

Everyone likes to get presents, and everyone likes to be thanked. So why is it so difficult to handle giving presents and thanking others in the workplace? The giving and receiving of gifts in the workplace is a delicate art. It should not be handled lightly; feelings are at stake.

I Didn't Get a Gift

Dear Jean,

What would you say about a supervisor who goes on vacation and comes back with a bag of gifts and hands them out to only some of the employees? This happened to me! I was one of the people who did not receive a gift. How would you feel if this had happened to you?

Reply:

Rotten. This is one of the most insensitive things I have ever heard. This bold and ugly gesture says more about your supervisor than it does you. There isn't much you can do, with the exception of asking her about her decision not to bring you a gift. Maybe she is angry with you and thought her passive-aggressive approach might shape you up. I hope you will consider asking her why you didn't receive a gift.

Different Salaries, Different Gifts?

Dear Jean,

With Christmas coming up, I'm starting to feel the stress of picking out gifts for my staff of seven. They all earn different salaries, have different tenure, and have different tastes. Is there a quick way to relieve me of all the mental gymnastics?

Reply:

There are plenty of business gifts that are in good taste. A few ideas are: monogrammed leather scrapbooks, luggage tags imprinted with their names and addresses, clocks, or subscriptions to popular magazines. Another fun idea is for you to go to one of the stores that design and assemble fancy gift baskets. You can pick out all the items yourself. Then they will shrink-wrap it and decorate it for the season. You can have nearly anything put in the basket, from popcorn to mugs to bath oil to chocolate. Your options are limited only by the size of the basket. That way you can personalize the gift. If you choose to spend a lot on some and not too much on others, it won't be as readily noticeable.

Fair and Equal Gift Giving

Dear Jean,

I work in a small company. On birthdays, it is a custom that we buy a gift and a card. Some of our staff members can't afford to give anything;

others can afford a large contribution. How do we equalize this?

Reply:

If there are people on your staff who can't afford a dollar or two, I suggest you change the custom. Buy one card and have everyone sign it. A card is enough, but if the lower-paid employees can contribute even pennies, then a small gift can be bought and everyone's name will go on the card. You're right in wanting to equalize this, because it is not fair for someone who makes $50,000 a year to pitch in the same amount as someone who makes $22,000.

Reward for Loyal Staff

Dear Jean,

I work for a large company and have nine people reporting to me. Our company has been through a particularly trying time this year, and my staff has been unusually loyal and productive. I'd like to buy each person a holiday gift. What can I give that is in good taste and doesn't cost a lot of money?

Reply:

Movie tickets are always a good bet. That way, a spouse, friend, or family member can enjoy your gift, too. Another idea is a book. Most every bookstore carries small hardback "gift books." Some are humorous and some carry light philosophical ideas and quotations.

A nice touch, either on the inside cover of the book or on the card which will accompany the movie ticket, would be for you to write a personal thank-you. Because this gift is meant as a thank-you it would be nice for you to add the personal touch of a written note. The personal note will be appreciated and kept and remembered.

Secretaries' Day

Dear Jean,

Regarding "Secretaries' Day," if our secretary is really not a secretary and is more of an administrative assistant, should we honor her that day and buy a gift?

Reply:

We have that same challenge in the Jean Kelley Personnel office because there are no actual secretaries. So I called Marsha Owen, certified professional secretary. She mentioned that the International Association of Administrative Professionals (formerly Professional Secretaries International) is attempting to shift the focus from lunch and a gift of flowers to an educational experience which the bosses underwrite. This year, IAAP promoted a workshop. The subject was "Professional Image and Creative Problem Solving." The workshop was a smashing success. So next year when April rolls around, there is an alternative to the tradition, one that will benefit you as well as your administrative support people. If IAAP isn't available in your community, you might pay for a continuing education course of her choosing at the local high school, college, or university.

Personal Gifts Cause Personal Problems

When I was in high school, a boss of mine gave me a 14-karat gold necklace. I was 17 at the time. He was 35, and I had a nagging notion that it was wrong to keep the necklace. I was not aware of any rules regarding accepting expensive gifts, but I was aware that if I kept the necklace, I would feel indebted.

For the next two days, I attempted to carry out my duties and to be as inconspicuous as possible while I figured out what to do about the gold cross and chain I was wearing.

I noticed that each time Mr. Moss passed me in the hall, he was acting less professional and more friendly. Our short conversations were becoming longer, and every time I looked up, he was there. He asked me to call him Michael. He asked me what kind of music I

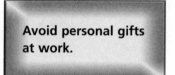

Avoid personal gifts at work.

liked and what my astrological sign was. Uh-oh, I thought, this is getting weird.

My direct supervisor, Linda, was a neat lady, so I decided to tell her what was going on. She said, "Oh no — the last time this happened, someone got fired." Linda told me that the month before I came to work, Mr. Moss gave another one of her trainees a piece of gold jewelry. Her parents found out about the bracelet and made her give it back to him.

He fired her.

As for me, I gave back the necklace, and I got fired, too.

An Impersonal Gift

Dear Jean,

One of the partners in my firm was especially helpful to me this year in obtaining a major account. Needless to say, I was pleased. I would like to remember her during the holidays for the generosity of her time and support. Because I am a married man, I don't want this gift to be at all personal. Can you think of anything I can give as a token of my appreciation?

Reply:

Something she could enjoy with her family or friends would be ideal. The first thing that comes to mind is a gift of food. Some of the nicer stores have gift items ranging from exotic jams to fine chocolate. They are elegantly wrapped for the season. A magnificent poinsettia is always in good taste. A gift certificate from a good bookstore would please many people. You may also wish to consider tickets to various types of entertainment being offered during the holiday season.

Watch out when you give an employee a gift that could be misconstrued as a personal present. There may be a jealous spouse just waiting to pounce.

A Benign Gift Is Best

Dear Jean,

My secretary's husband is jealous. I mean really jealous. He brings her to work, takes her to lunch every day, checks in midmorning and midafternoon, and picks her up promptly at five.

It is customary for me to recognize my secretary at Christmas, and I'm in a quandary as to what to give her. What do you think?

Reply:

I think that you are going to have a problem regarding this jealousy sooner or later, but that's another question and answer.

As far as Christmas goes, pick out something that both she and her husband can enjoy. Movie tickets, ball-game tickets, maybe tickets to a play or ballet. Another safe bet is a gift certificate to their favorite restaurant. And remember, no diamond bracelets!

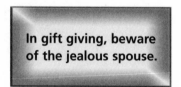

In gift giving, beware of the jealous spouse.

Another Jealous Husband

Dear Jean,

My administrative assistant has a very jealous husband. I would like to get her something special for Christmas. Last year, I bought her a pen-and-pencil set. I later heard from another source that her husband was upset about the gift. Can you imagine? Upset about a pen-and-pencil set? Where do I go from here?

Reply:

If her husband was upset about a pen-and-pencil set, he is either nuts or has had a past experience that caused his jealousy. Not knowing the complete history of your working relationship makes this one a hard question to answer. What about a three-day weekend? Certainly he wouldn't take offense at that.

Not everyone agrees with this idea. Read this response I got to my answer.

Dear Jean,

I'm not a jealous husband, but if my wife were to get a day off work, I might wonder if the boss was hoping she would spend it with him. Last year, I found out that my wife had gotten several extra afternoons off. All I know is that she never told me about them, and I've wondered ever since where and with whom she spent them. Now I ask her specifically what her hours are going to be each week. From now on, if her boss gives her a gift, I'd just as soon he stick with the kind that can be gift-wrapped.

Reply:

*Are you **sure** you aren't a "jealous husband"?*

Client Gifts

Clients and customers are our lifeblood. It is natural to acknowledge them whenever we can. However, sometimes this can be just as difficult as giving a gift within your own office.

Client's Wife Is Pregnant

Dear Jean,

Last week while having lunch with a client, I learned that his wife is five months pregnant with their first child. I'd like to mark the occasion with a gift, but I'm not sure what would be in good taste. This is not a large client, but I really enjoy our business relationship. What kind of gift should I buy? Should I give them the gift now, or wait until the baby is born?

Reply:

There is a certain advantage to presenting a gift now. You have a better chance of their remembering the gift and who gave it to them. My favorite all-purpose baby gift is a picture frame. Every couple takes a lot of pictures of their first baby, and one can be found to fit any budget. The cost ranges from $15 to $50. Anything from Lucite to silver plate would be a good pick.

My Client Can't Accept Gifts

Dear Jean,

I'm a marketing manager for a large distribution company and my major client cannot accept gifts from suppliers. I want to recognize this relationship and thank the client for the business. What do I do?

Reply:

This is not unusual. Many large companies are adamant about avoiding anything that hints of "kickbacks." So what about giving something even more personal than a gift? Because this is your major client, you probably know a lot about the people and their interests, both career and personal. Why not clip out an article from a magazine every month that will be of interest to them? It will show that you care about them as people. If you don't subscribe to zillions of magazines, just buy one or two business magazines now and then. Most marketing people don't take the time to do something this personal. This will make you pleasantly conspicuous.

Gifts for Bosses

They pay our salary, give us a nice place to work and, we hope, support us in our efforts to advance. Bosses get very little acknowledgment for all the things they do for their employees, and they need it as much as the employees do.

A Gift for a Great Boss

Dear Jean,

I am a 25-year-old female. I work for a large insurance company. This is the first job I have had where I can't wait to get to work every day.

My boss is a prince of a guy. He treats me with dignity and is constantly encouraging me. His birthday is coming up next month. Should I buy him a nice gift to show my appreciation?

Reply:

This man probably has everything he needs, but he can always use more appreciation from his employees. A handwritten thank-you note on plain stationery or a note card is the perfect way to show your appreciation. Send it today!

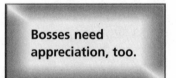

Bosses need appreciation, too.

With regard to gift giving: Unless you know that gift giving is the norm at your company, I would suggest that you give or send him a lighthearted birthday card.

Even if gift giving is done at your company, I would suggest that you, as a new employee, avoid anything that will give people an opportunity to talk. A 25-year-old female who buys her boss a gift will, unfortunately, cause raised eyebrows. No matter how innocent your gesture, there are a lot of people around who have really boring lives. Avoid giving them fantasy fodder.

Not everyone agrees.

Dear Jean,

I don't agree that a young woman can't give her male boss a present. I was in a sort of similar situation and bought my boss a nice plant for his office. I didn't make a big show of giving it to him; I just dropped it by his office on his birthday with a "Happy Birthday" sort of thank-you note. I know he felt appreciated and I don't think anyone thought anything of it. There was nothing sleazy about it and I'm glad I was able to show him my appreciation.

My reply:

Of course, all offices are different and a nice plant might be the perfect gift for some bosses.

So maybe your boss isn't exactly a "prince of a guy" as in the preceding question. Maybe your boss is thoroughly repulsive. Does that make it OK (or safe) to ignore him when Boss's Day comes around?

Gift for Unliked Boss

Dear Jean,

What do I do for "Boss's Day" when I don't particularly care for my boss, but other people around me are doing things for their bosses?

Reply,

Plan A: I'm sure you've figured out that not acknowledging the day will make a big statement. How big a statement do you want to make? If you want to keep a low profile, avoid crossing your own value system, and not make waves, then a nonsentimental card will do.

Plan B: Get a new boss.

Plan C: Get everyone together to buy a gift for the office in all the bosses' names. You contribute your share and when the "boss from hell" leaves, you still get to use that great new cappuccino machine.

The Importance of Saying "Thank You"

Write a Thank-you Anyway

Dear Jean,

My birthday was last week. My department had a party for me. Someone I hate (and for good reason) gave me a small gift of food. I don't even like the food. Do I have to write a thank-you note to this person?

Reply:

Liking the gift or liking the sender has very little to do with the gesture of thanks. Civility in the workplace is underrated. It's nice to write a thank-you, no matter who sent the gift, no matter what the gift is.

Thanking the Boss's Mom

Dear Jean,

Our boss lives with his mother, and this sweet old lady is always sending cookies or cake to the office. We love to nibble her "offerings" when we go to the break room. Should we send the bossman's mother something?

Reply:

Of course. A flowering plant and a thank-you note would be an ideal gift. It would also be nice to remember her for these kind gestures during the holiday season and, if practical, on her birthday. Aside from pleasing her, it will please your boss, too — and you can't go wrong pleasing your boss.

"Thanks" from My Spouse

Dear Jean,

I am a senior manager for a large public company. Recently, my company had a meeting in Vail, Colorado. My husband was invited to join me on the trip. We had a wonderful time. Should I write a thank-you to the president, or should it be written by my husband?

Reply:

How nice of your company to include your spouse! Because you were the person to receive the invitation from the company, it would be best for you to respond on behalf of you and your husband.

Have you ever been in a thankless job? Maintenance staff and cleaning staff typically get very little thanks. Their work is physical, and everyone they talk to throughout the day is having problems.

Thank Your Cleaning People, Too

Dear Jean,

The people who clean our office do a great job. I'm not the boss, but can I do something to show them I appreciate their work?

Reply:

How nice to receive your letter! Let me tell you what I do in a case such as this.

We have unusually good maintenance in our building. No matter what the problem is, the staff is there with a solution within minutes. Not only is their response time excellent, they always seem to be happy to help.

Every year during the holiday season, I give each of them a care package of baked goodies. I belong to an ethnic group with rich holiday traditions. A part of what gives the season meaning to me is preparing cookies and candy from recipes that have been handed down for generations. A gift like this would be perfect.

If baking is not one of your talents, you can do what a New York City friend of mine does every year for his doorman. He gives a nice tip.

Maybe your style is neither to bake nor to tip. If that is the case, a well-thought-out thank-you note or card is a nice touch. Even better, write a letter about the office cleaning people and send it to their boss. That way your grateful regard, on paper, might help them up the career ladder in the maintenance field.

Many people agonize over thank-you notes. This is not a good enough reason not to write a note. People appreciate getting the note so much that they are too busy being thankful to you to doubt your motives or your sincerity. Just do it.

Will She Doubt My Sincerity?

Dear Jean,

I wrote to my daughter's dance teacher a special thank-you note after her recital in June. It was a very sincere, from-the-heart note about how much I appreciated all the contributions she was making to my daughter's self-esteem, self-respect, character, etc. It was a very special note for me to write. I also wrote a thank-you note to another teacher in the school, just a general thank-you, nothing special.

The special teacher has thanked me for the note and expressed how much it meant to her. She was very touched, and that made me feel I had accomplished what I intended with the note. I had not seen the other teacher until yesterday, and she thanked me for the thank-you note. My problem is that she thanked me for her note in front of the special teacher. I am just sick about this because I do not want her to think that the note I sent her was not sincere and from my heart. Do I write her again and explain? Do I talk to her about the note I sent the other teacher, or do I just do nothing?

Reply:

No need to make a big deal of this. No doubt the special teacher knows you didn't write the same thing to the other teacher. If you are still feeling odd about this in a month, it would be all right to write another note, especially if you have observed something in your daughter that was directly attributable to the special teacher.

Often I am asked if it is proper to write a thank-you card after having received a thank-you gift. It depends on the gift. If the gift is tickets to the ballet, yes, write a note. If the gift is a box of

> **Write a thank-you note for a thank-you gift? It depends.**

candy, a note may not be necessary. If you feel thankful, go with your hunch. Write a thank-you note.

A Thank-you for a Thank-you

Dear Jean,

I am one of those people who might be called a workaholic. I'm the type who gets to work early and stays late. I love what I do. No challenge is too great. Occasionally, I'm rewarded for my "above and beyond the call of duty" work and I receive dinner for two or symphony tickets. Should I write a thank-you note for a thank-you gift?

Reply:

I'm so glad you asked that question. I'm wondering when you last received a personal thank-you note. How did you feel? Great, I'll bet. Pass it on! I strongly believe that everyone wants to feel important — the way you felt when your boss handed you the tickets. Because thank-you notes are never in bad taste, I hope you'll write them often!

In this high-tech society, the personal touch has sadly given way to faxes, e-mail, voice mail, express mail, and the more-than-ever-present telephone. That's really too bad, because there's something deeply touching about a personal, handwritten thank-you note. In many cases, they are more impressive than a gift. Anyone can buy a gift.

Recently, I received a thank-you letter from a woman I had helped to find a job nine years ago. I want to stress the word *helped* because, in fact, I did not find her the employment she desired. I had not had any contact with her since that time. She lives in Dallas and is in an excellent upper-management job.

In her letter, she thanked me for the personal interest I had in her and told me that my believing in her had made a difference in her life. The letter blew me away.

When was the last time you received a handwritten thank-you note? What did you do with it? Did you save it?

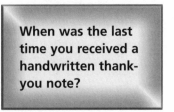

When was the last time you received a handwritten thank-you note?

I save all the thank-you notes and special cards I receive during the year. I put them in a file folder and label the file by the year. Whenever I feel gloomy or when I want to spend a rainy afternoon alone, I go through my old cards and letters. I have long forgotten about most of the gifts I have received in the last few years, but I still have ALL the letters and cards.

When the mail comes to my office, I speedily run through all the items hoping to find a small envelope with handwriting on it. I open those first. The busier I perceive the senders to be, the more impressed I am to receive cards from them.

Thank-you notes are written for all kinds of reasons. Brian Tracy, a popular public speaker and business consultant, says, "You will double your income in one year if you will write 25 thank-yous a week." Can you find 25 things to be grateful for every week?

One of the best reasons I have heard for writing thank-yous and notes of congratulations is that it makes the other person feel important. Who doesn't like to feel important? Another very good reason to take pen in hand is that it's just nice manners.

People continuously ask me, "What should I thank people for?" I say, *"Everything!"*

Points to Remember

☐ It's not the thought that counts, it's the gift that counts. Choose wisely.

☐ When you are given an inappropriate gift, give it back.

☐ Stay away from giving gifts that are too personal.

☐ When giving a gift to a married person, why not choose something their spouse will enjoy, too?

☐ A handwritten thank-you note is a great way to show appreciation to your boss, or anyone.

☐ When you receive a gift, send a thank-you no matter who sent the gift and no matter what the gift is.

☐ Civility makes the workplace more pleasant.

☐ In some cases its good to write a thank-you note for a thank-you gift.

Dressing — Up or Down?

You will never get a second chance at a first impression. If you don't think this is true, picture yourself with appendicitis. You are in the emergency room and the doctor appears. His hair looks like the crown of the Statue of Liberty and it is chartreuse. Even though he is wearing the traditional white coat, his left eyebrow is pierced. Will you give this doctor a second chance at a first impression?

John T. Malloy wrote a very successful book, *Dress for Success*. It changed my life. Still in print, the book is as meaningful today as it was when I read it the first time. After reading the book, I embraced his research 100 percent. Malloy maintained that people responded to one another based in large part on what they wore. He said a person's profession, level of education, and socioeconomic level could be identified by choices of clothing, shoes, and accessories. His basic advice was to stay conservative and traditional and to buy clothing that was well constructed with classic fabrics.

You will never get a second chance at a first impression.

It fascinated me that a stranger could tell whether I was a legal secretary, a salesperson, or an executive by my clothes. The idea that a stranger could tell whether my father was a doctor or factory worker fascinated me even more. I had so much fun fantasizing about his theory, I decided to do my own research.

I dressed up in different outfits and headed for the airport terminal. I would put a big smile on my face and ask people if they would help me with my research. When they said yes, I gave them a brief form to fill out. The multiple-choice questions ranged from what my father did for a living to the last year of school I completed.

WOW, what an education! The effect clothing had on Joe and Jane Public amazed me. One of my experiments included a long, full, curly black wig. Along with the wig, I chose a denim miniskirt, pink tube top, and pink blouse tied at the waist. I wore white snakeskin high heels and white anklets trimmed with lace. Believe me, I didn't have to see the responses on the forms to know what people thought. Their reactions were enough. On the elevator, mothers were pulling their children close. The reactions from men were even more fun. They would do one of two things. Either they would give me a flirtatious look or they would avoid eye contact at any cost.

At work, the rules are simple. Look the part. How you look and act will determine your speed up the corporate ladder. Dress for the next position higher, where you would like to be. For example, if you are a receptionist who would like to be an executive assistant, you'd better get busy with the corporate wardrobe. Pick out someone who looks like "upwardly mobile" and pattern your dress after that — most likely you will start moving up, too.

Proper Business Attire

Now we know that corporate dress is important, but what exactly is "proper business attire"? The lines are fuzzy here, so if that is your question, you are not alone.

Wear a Suit

Dear Jean,

When you are looking for a job in a corporate office, do you still need to wear a suit to apply? I'm a new grad and I don't own a suit. I don't even own pantyhose, but I'm sure I can get a pair of those. The suit? I don't think that I can afford that. Can you help me?

Reply:

The suited look is still the best no-risk choice of clothing for an interview. I suggest that out of respect to the interviewer and the corporation, it's good taste to wear a business suit, even if you know that the company has a policy of casual dress every day. Don't pick a plain, three-button, boxy business suit. Pick an interesting suit in a becoming color. Coordinate your blouse and accessories to match. Anyone can pick a boring, boxy suit. Let your personality shine through a bit.

If your sights are set on a corporate management position, you will not only need a suit for interviews, you will need a couple of suits to wear to work, or at the very least, a nice, conservative dress with a jacket. You will need a couple of closed-toe, low-heeled pumps. Even if you go to work for a "casual-dress company," I would still suggest that your own style of casual includes a couple of blazers and khaki slacks.

Like it or not, people who can see you will always judge you by what you wear. Even if you're convinced that you don't judge people by their appearance, go to the mall and tell me what kind of impression you get from the girl with the purple and orange striped hair, leather-spiked necklace, Spandex tube top, and pierced tongue. Can you suspend judgment? Nope? Neither can I.

You mentioned that you can't afford to buy a suit. You can't afford not to.

How Should I Dress at Work?

Dear Jean,

What is the appropriate way to dress at work? I work in an office.

Reply:

Things are changing as far as dress codes in the workplace. Many companies are going to casual days on Fridays. The words corporate casual usually mean slacks and jackets or slacks and a nice shirt or sweater. Some companies wear jeans on casual days. A few companies are wearing casual clothing all the time.

So if this is a new job you are starting, ask about the dress code before you decide what to wear to work. Often companies have a written dress code that you can refer to. For a woman, a dress is always appropriate. Wear a dress or suit until you know about the company dress code. For a man in a management or administrative position, it is good to wear a tie unless you know the dress code is casual.

Valerie Jacobi is a good example of corporate dress. She works in a "techie" area of a large international company. They have no face-to-face contact with customers. She is a customer service representative. The culture is *"business casual"* every day, not just on Friday. The people around her take the *casual* word seriously — very seriously. Her co-workers wear jeans, tennis shoes, and T-shirts. Valerie wears khaki pants, loafers, and tailored shirts.

Valerie's seemingly unimportant choices have made a major impact on how management perceives her. She received a promotion within the first year of her employment. Granted, she had to be smart to receive the promotion, but she works with plenty of other smart people. The thing that made the difference was that she was perceived as being a little more professional than her colleagues.

Corporate Casual

Dear Jean,

I am a 30-year-old marketing staff assistant. I work for a Fortune 500 company. Recently, our top salesperson landed a huge account. As a result, I have been invited to celebrate at the home of our executive vice president. The memo requested that our attire be "corporate casual." What exactly is corporate casual? We don't even have casual Fridays at our company, so I'm clueless.

Reply:

Corporate casual means different things to different companies. Usually however, it means no jeans.

Since the party is not during work hours and it is at an executive's home, your best bet is to go "suburban casual." Wear a blazer or a sweater and slacks. As a rule, I would suggest this to both men and women. If you get to the party and find that you are overdressed, all you have to do is take off a layer.

My basic philosophy: It's better to overdress than to underdress. Levi Strauss has great up-to-date information on casual dress. You can view it at www.levistrauss.com.

It is crucial to have a suitable wardrobe. Borrow the money if you must. There are several economic ways to acquire a good business wardrobe. One of the best retail options for women is by catalog. I suggest Chadwick's of Boston. The address is P.O. Box 1600, Taunton, MA 02780-0975. Ask the company to put you on its mailing list.

An economical way for both men and women to dress is to stay on top of the inventory at a few good secondhand consignment stores. You can pick up some unbelievable bargains. Just make sure you stay conservative in your taste.

Casual Dress Codes

Stuffy business attire seems to be losing some of its popularity in business. More and more offices are allowing their employees to relax a little, especially on Fridays. In some companies, Friday attire will consist of jeans and a T-shirt, even tennis shoes. Four million trees worldwide have lost their lives because of memos on dress codes.

There is not one singular definition of casual, but I'll attempt to set the guidelines: For men, nice khakis or gray wool (tropical or flannel) slacks which can be accompanied by a navy blazer. The blazer can be double- or single-breasted with gold- or silver-colored buttons. Cardigan sweaters and sweater vests are a good bet, too. The shirts that make the list are button-down cotton with no tie. Short-sleeved polo-type shirts are acceptable as well.

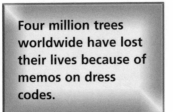

Four million trees worldwide have lost their lives because of memos on dress codes.

People judge shoes nearly as strictly as a handshake. Well-maintained bucks and loafers are the only shoes that qualify. Shoes should match the belt. Tennis shoes and sandals are definitely out.

Studies indicate that women may be negatively affected by casual dress codes. Women have enough challenge being taken seriously in the workplace. Spaghetti-strap Ts and barefoot sandals don't help. Wearing color combinations that appear in men's casual dress are best. Gray, beige, and taupe test well. Stay away from big floral prints. Khakis and chinos are best with a natural-fabric shirt, nice belt, and bucks or loafers. Long skirts and shirts in natural fabrics with closed-toe flats or loafers work, too.

As far as shoes go, clogs, moccasins, and cowboy boots are bad choices. As a general rule for women and men, the shoe should match the hem of the pants or dress or be darker. In other words, white shoes are not a good investment — ever!

Starting Casual Friday Dress

Dear Jean,

How do I get the owner of our company to let us have a casual Friday every week?

Reply:

If your boss wanted you to dress casually, you would know it by now. You have a sales job on your hands. Most bosses aren't opposed to corporate casual dress now and then. What they fear is sloppy, unwashed, or provocative casual dress.

To save time, give some thought to what casual dress means to you and to the people with whom you work. Write down your requests in a proposal. Stay conservative at first; for example, don't ask to wear open-toed sandals with bare feet.

Here's an idea that will work about 50 percent of the time. Your boss probably has a favorite not-for-profit cause. Ask if you can "buy" a casual dress day every Friday by contributing to that favorite charity. Somewhere between three and five dollars makes sense.

Sell this idea as a win-win solution. It is.

Should I Just Start Wearing "Summer Dress"?

Dear Jean,

No one has said anything about "summer dress" in our office, so we are all buttoned up and hosed down, so to speak. What do you think would happen if I wore Bermuda shorts to the office? Do you think I could get away with it, or should I break down and check with the boss first?

Reply:

It's a good thing to check with the boss before breaking with any kind of tradition. I once heard that "the best surprise is no surprise." This would apply here.

She Won't Let Us Dress Casual, Too

Dear Jean,

Everyone at our company is dressing "summertime casual." Everyone, that is, except people in my particular office. Our supervisor is a sour old maid if ever I saw one. She insists that we "dress for success." She wants us in skirted garments with jackets, pantyhose, and closed-toe shoes. I think it's just because we are seven women. If there were a man in our group, I'll bet he would be wearing jeans and a short-sleeved shirt and we would be wearing slacks, shorts, and sundresses like the rest of the company. Should I ignore her and get myself comfortable?

Reply:

It sounds as if your boss is not keeping current with the casual Friday trend. She may eventually come around to your way of thinking, but it won't be overnight. The switch from traditional to casual is quite a stretch.

It's fine to try to sell her on the casual idea, but start small. Ask if your office can have a casual Friday now and then. If that turns out to be successful, ask if your office can have a casual Friday every week.

As for what would happen to your departmental dress code if there were a man in your group, you may be right. It's best, though, to leave speculation to the people who get paid to speculate — the stockbrokers.

Some employers are so conventional or formal that you may be lucky to get an occasional dress-down day. You may not *ever* reach the "casual summer dress" or "casual everyday" status. I was a slow one to come around, too, but I am now an enthusiastic supporter of casual Fridays. On weeks when we surpass quota, we go all out. We even wear jeans!

It Isn't Fair!

Bosses are particular about dress codes. Sometimes different codes apply to different people. Although this may not seem fair to you, life is not fair. The boss is the boss.

Shouldn't We All Dress the Same?

Dear Jean,

I am a receptionist at a pretty big company. When I was hired, I was told that I must always wear professional dress, no matter what. I don't mind wearing hose and heels every day, but everyone else is so casual. Some even wear jeans. I kind of feel out of place. I may be mistaken here, but I thought that everyone in a company had to follow the same dress-code policy.

Reply:

It usually is the case that everyone has to adhere to the same dress code, but it apparently isn't the case at your company. Since you were informed of this when you were hired, at least you knew what you were getting into. Many companies rely on their receptionist to present a professional appearance to visitors.

As a receptionist, you are the director of first impressions. Your appearance and your voice form the image your firm shows to the outside world. I am happy to hear that you don't mind dressing up for work.

No matter how casual the dress gets in our country, one fact remains. People who are extremely well-groomed and have their own sense of style are taken seriously and get more promotions. Nido Qubein, author, consultant, and one of the best-dressed men in corporate America, says, "The only difference between high achievers and average achievers is that the high achievers do the little things that the average achievers are not willing to do."

P.S.: Someone trained specifically in employment law can tell you if all employees have to follow the same dress code. But if I were you, I wouldn't spend much time worrying about it.

Do I Have to Wear a Tie?

Dear Jean,

I work in a medium-sized advertising firm. I am the senior manager in my department and have been with this company for nine years. Up until now, our department has been rather laid back and casual. Because of that, I have never had to wear a suit to work.

Last week, out of the clear blue, my boss told me that our casual dress was a thing of the past and that I would have to wear a tie in the office. I immediately replied, "I will wear a tie the day you make all the women wear a tie."

This was four days ago. I am still furious and I have not complied. My boss gives me a condescending glance every morning, but has not brought up the subject again.

Reply:

Have you thought about who you are talking to? Granted, your boss may have a lack of tact, but he is your boss.

You may have won the battle, but I don't know what good it will do you because soon this topic will return to the front burner. It is to your advantage to be the one to bring up the subject. The best way to open the conversation about casual versus dressy is to say, "Hey, I'm uncomfortable about the dress-code discussion you and I had last week. I'd like to know if we can talk again." This time, listen. Listen carefully. Remember who you're talking to!

After your boss is completely through with his request, verify whether you heard him correctly or not by paraphrasing what he just said. Then it will be your turn to talk.

Keep a cool head and state your well-thought-out ideas. Stop and listen to your boss again. Take turns until you are both fully "heard." Then take action on what you've agreed upon. By the way, count your blessings. You may have to wear a tie and suit at your next job.

Men Should Be Allowed to Wear Sandals, Too

Dear Jean,

The women in our department get to wear sandals with no socks or hose. I think the men should be able to wear sandals with no socks, but the boss said, "No hairy toes in the office." Do you think that is fair?

Reply:

The company is allowed to dictate the dress code, and even though the situation you mentioned is not fair, it is the request of your boss, and your compliance with

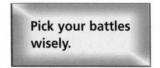

Pick your battles wisely.

your boss's wishes will determine your future with the company where you are working.

Learn to pick your battles wisely. There are many serious issues during a day's business. Avoid making a big deal out of something that won't amount to much in terms of your career. Save your energy. You're gonna need it.

Do I Have to Let Everyone Wear Shorts?

Dear Jean,

Very soon, the shorts/no shorts on casual-day arrangement will rear its head again. A few of the young women who work for me look great in shorts. Others look gross in any kind of short pants. When I say shorts are OK for the male workers must I, or should I, specifically exclude women?

Reply:

Excluding any one group from wearing shorts will net you a lot of trouble.

You could easily have a rebellion on your hands, and while your employees are rebelling, no work will be getting done.

The best way to approach a dress code is to ask the same thing of the men and the women. In other words, everyone wears shorts or no one wears shorts. Most companies put restrictions on the length of shorts. The term walking shorts seems to be a widely used term for what is appropriate at the office.

Sometime when you are really bored, your work is caught up, and you don't mind a lawsuit, here's an idea. Send a memo stating that all the people who look bad in shorts must not wear them at the office. Name them all.

It's Time to Change Your Look

When it comes to choosing the right look for the office, some people just don't get it. What they don't realize is the effect that their "look" has on their career.

She Looks So Sloppy

Dear Jean,

My administrative assistant is the sweetest person who ever lived. She is also extremely competent. I inherited her when her boss left the company.

There is only one problem. She dresses so sloppily that I hate to have her receiving my guests. I don't want to hurt her feelings, but her upward mobility will be drastically reduced by her appearance.

Reply:

If you sincerely care about her, you're the best person to tell her. This will be the greatest gift you could ever give her — a key to her future. You will need to be specific. Don't leave anything to chance. You might even want a trusted friend to help her shop. Be sure to "inspect what you expect." The days when she looks especially professional, comment on her appearance. Soon, she will learn what you like and don't like in the area of professional dress.

About 12 years ago, we had a young woman at our company who was bright, talented, and wore big, white, scuffed-up spiked-heeled pumps. To make things worse, she occasionally wore beaded and sequined dresses with those big white pumps. Everyone liked Dennie. She had nice manners, good grammar, and a personality that wore well with all types of people.

There was just the one problem, and somebody needed to tell her. I was that somebody. One day, I asked Dennie to lunch and I explained how her career would be enhanced if she learned to dress in a more conservative manner. She was grateful for my honesty and really felt that I wanted the best for her.

Luckily, one of our former employees was in the makeup and fashion-jewelry business. Dennie worked alongside her for several months and looked up to her. I put the two of them together, and the rest is history. She is now the marketing manager of a bank in Pennsylvania.

Bald and Beautiful

Dear Jean,

My office contemporary is a nice-looking guy about my age. I like him a lot (I'm married, we're just good friends) and he tells me about the lack of women in his life. He's bald, but he combs his hair up from the back and sides in such an odd way it makes him look like a geek. Do I dare tell him that he'd be a thousand times more appealing if he would just let his bald head shine? I think it might even help him move up in the company.

Reply:

He wears his hair that way because he thinks it's more attractive than going natural. It's a "Samson" thing. Hey, I'm with you. There is nothing wrong with an honest bald head. Chances are if you ask 100 women, the overwhelming majority of them would agree.

As for moving up in the company, I'd like to think hiring decisions are made by qualifications and not by the cut of someone's tresses, but I'm not 100 percent sure that is always the case. You may be one of the only people in his life who can and will tell him the truth.

Keep a straight face and tell him this: "Authorities have come to the conclusion that baldness is caused by an overabundance of testosterone — and we all know what that means." This is the old ploy of starting with the "goodest" news before you get to the good news — bald is natural, and who can quarrel with nature?

I applaud your courage. Let it shine. Let it shine. Let it shine.

Spiked Heels

Dear Jean,

I'm a salesperson with a national firm. I do pretty well, but the woman they call their "star" salesperson is making me crazy. She gets all kinds of privileges and she looks like a slut. Jean, I always wear a black, blue, or gray suit and I am careful about my makeup, hair, nails, etc. For some reason, I sure don't get a trip to Bermuda. What should I do — shorten my skirts and lower my neckline?

Reply:

I'm assuming that she earned those trips to Bermuda by winning contests. Something I read recently said that we all have access to a pair of magic magnifying glasses. When we put them on, whatever we focus on increases. If we look at the problem, the problem increases. If we look at the solution, the solution increases.

My best advice to you is to look at the solution. What is it you could be doing to increase your personal production? Do you need to make more calls? Do you need a refresher on closing the sale? Do you qualify your prospects properly? Do you have excellent time-management skills?

*If she can be the national sales star, so can you. Don't spend any more time thinking about her. On the other hand, if you **know** beyond a shadow of a doubt that the absolute **only** reason she is the national sales star is her provocative dress and that **none** of her success is due to her sales ability, shorten your skirts, buy some Spandex, and start wearing outlandish makeup. Why stop there? Add a see-through blouse and a pair of five-inch heels.*

Well-endowed Worker

Dear Jean,

One of my female employees who is very well endowed often wears clothing that is low cut and somewhat revealing. To me, this borders on poor taste, and it tends to be very distracting to other employees and clients. How can I broach this subject and put an end to this provocative situation?

Reply:

I agree. It borders on bad taste, but my picture of "somewhat revealing" may be quite different from your perception and your clients' perceptions. There are appropriate ways of dressing in corporate U.S. It is in equally bad taste for a man to wear his shirt unbuttoned, showing off his hairy chest and tattoos.

Before you say or do anything, examine her sales record. Is she your top salesperson? Unless you are getting customer complaints, you may be on legal shaky ground. You may want to consider a formal written dress code. And remember, the policy must be written for everyone, men as well as women.

Body Art

Although dress codes are becoming more lenient, it's still important to be neatly dressed and well-groomed. Green and pink hair may work in some offices, but in most it won't. Your best bet is to stick with the basics. In other words, make sure your hair color is a variation of what could grow out of a normal person's head.

As for tattoos and body piercings, yes, they do make you stand out from the crowd. However, if they are visible, especially on the face or hands, they can severely limit your opportunities. Think carefully before adding pictures or extra holes to your body. If you're still not a believer consider this. I have a 25-year-old friend who has already spent nearly $4,000 trying to get her tattoo removed. You don't have to be old and wrinkled to think they are not cool.

Tongue Piercing

Dear Jean,

My tongue is pierced and I wear what is called a "barbell" in it. Recently, I went on an interview which resulted in a job offer at a retail store. There is one problem, though. The man who hired me told me that I would have to take my barbell out while at work. I don't think that is fair. People have their ears pierced and they don't have to take out their earrings for work.

Reply:

Your new boss has the obligation to the store owners to make a profit and his job depends on it. Part of his task in making a profit is to create a maximum buying mood for the customer. Unless he is selling tongue jewelry, he may think that your tongue jewelry will be distracting to your customers, maybe even disgusting.

How we choose to adorn ourselves is an unspoken statement about who we are and what we value. Dress codes are a part of nearly every profit-seeking company. It is not unusual for a company to request that shirttails be tucked in, that socks be worn with shoes, and that skirts be a certain length. Appropriate dress varies from one company to the next, but I'll bet "barbells" are not acceptable in many of the companies in the Midwest or Southwest. I understand dress codes are somewhat looser on the East and West coasts.

Dress codes do infringe on our lives, but think of it this way. What would it be like for you to go to a lawyer's office, to be met by someone who is wearing a black leather jacket with a skull and crossbones on it?

Eyebrow Ring

Dear Jean,

When I graduated from college, my girl-friend bought me an eyebrow ring as a

> **You will be judged by how you look.**

graduation present. I have never taken it off since the day she went with me to get it done. At the present time, I am interviewing for a job in an office. I am a software designer and typically won't ever have to talk to customers. Do you think it is OK for me to wear this ring on my inter-views? It is really a part of who I am.

Reply:

You can wear the ring if you know that the interviewer also has body piercings or if you know for sure that at least 15 percent of the employees are also wearing body jewelry. Otherwise, leave it at home.

Will a Tattoo Keep Me from Getting a Job?

Dear Jean,

I want to get a tattoo on my ankle. I think they look great and several of my friends have them. My parents told me that I'll never get a job if I get a tattoo. Is that really true?

Reply:

No, that is not true. Having a tattoo on your ankle does not mean that you will never get a job. A tattoo on your face, neck, or hands, though, may restrict you. It depends on the company. In some companies, purple and yellow striped hair is strictly taboo; in other companies, it may be the rage. The difference depends on many things, such as customer contact, the age of the president, and the type of company.

A few years ago, if someone had told me that I would have people working in my office who have tattoos, I would have told them that they were wacko. The picture I had in my mind of women with tattoos was very different from the reality of two very professional women in my office who have roses on their ankles.

No Tattoos

Dear Jean,

I have been begging for a tattoo, and for Christmas my parents said I could have one. They gave me the money and I was all ready to go. Someone mentioned to my boss that I was getting a tattoo and he said I couldn't. I am wondering if he can fire me if I get a tattoo. He didn't say that he would, but he's very unhappy.

Reply:

He could fire you. I'm not saying that it is right for your boss to be able to tell you what you can put on your body, but in some companies there are policies called dress codes.

I'm assuming you are wanting your tattoo in a not-so-discreet place or you wouldn't have written. A big butterfly on your cheek is very different from a big rose on your hip. You do need to take into consideration your boss's position on this as you are making your decision. How important is your job to you?

Hair-color Discrimination

Dear Jean

I applied for a job recently and was told that I didn't get the job because my hair is eggplant (they mistakenly called it purple). I don't think that's right. Can they really discriminate against me because they don't like my hair?

Reply:

Yes. Generally speaking, in a business office, acceptable hair colors would be natural-looking variations of blonde, brown, black, gray, and red. Any color outside the basic five is considered to be distracting. There are some businesses where eggplant would fly, but my suggestion is to stick with the basics.

Next time you go to your closet to pick out what you are going to wear to work, take a moment to ask yourself a few questions. What are your goals at work that day and in the future? What is your corporate culture really like? Are you in sync? Do your clothes portray the image you want to portray at the office (not necessarily the image you see as the "real" you)?

The way you dress at work will have a huge impact on how capable your supervisors perceive you. Be careful when choosing your at-work wardrobe. It can be the catapult that shoots you into a better position just as easily as it can be the weapon that shoots you down.

Points to Remember

☐ You will never get a second chance at a first impression.

☐ Learn what "proper business attire" is at your particular company.

☐ "Business casual" is different at every company.

☐ "Corporate casual" usually means no jeans.

☐ Pick your battles wisely.

☐ How you choose to adorn yourself is an unspoken statement about who you are. You will be judged by how you look.

☐ Tattoos and body piercings may not keep you from ever getting a job, but sometimes they can determine what kind of job you get.

Bosses from Hell

8

Have you ever had a boss who made you say to yourself "How did she ever get to be a boss?" or "Someone was asleep at the wheel when he got promoted." More than half of the bosses in the US are unprepared and untrained to be bosses. Some of them could even benefit from a little psychological help. Have you ever worked for one?

That said, here's the deal. Your boss is your boss. That means your boss has a right to tell you what to do and you have an obligation to do it. Your boss does not have a right to abuse you, but he or she does have a right to give you directions. Abuse, by the way, is not nagging, griping, or delegation.

In some cases where you have a good relationship with your boss, you might get by with objecting to the method by which you do the work. But the bottom line is, you will be doing the work.

If your boss asks you to do something that is illegal or immoral, you have a decision to make. A word of caution here. Anytime your boss asks you to do something that gives you a queasy feeling inside, spruce up your resume. Unless you are enthusiastic about illegal or immoral action, you are on your way out.

Having worked with more than 20,000 people who were looking for new jobs, I've heard at least half a million reasons why people have left their jobs, so I am an expert on bosses from hell. I've even *been* a boss from hell, and there's more about that in another chapter.

I started my career in the personnel industry before there was language to describe much of the behavior we now consider improper. Employment law in the mid-1970s started a huge wave of change that is still gaining momentum. Sweeping changes were made in the way companies screened candidates for employment. In the early '70s, it was not at all unusual for an employer with a job opening to request a woman with no small children or a woman who was on the pill.

A man or woman who had had major surgeries or was on medication was considered an absenteeism risk and was usually not hired. This included women who had had hysterectomies.

Almost all bosses were male in the early '70s, and distasteful requests were frequent. For instance, an employer might ask for a woman who could travel with him. That would require that she be single, of course. Our clients would ask for a woman with short skirts, claiming their customers demanded sexy attire. In my first month of employment in the personnel business, a man called us looking for a new secretary. He wanted a young girl who wore "see-through" blouses.

Worse yet, clients would ask us to be sure to send only "white girls." And then they would say something like, "It's not me who wants only whites; as a matter of fact, some of my best friends are black. It's my customers who are demanding white employees, and I have an obligation to do whatever my customers ask. As you know, Jean, the customer is always right." (Yeah, right.)

When it comes to sexual harassment, there is little comparison between then and now. I'm not saying sexual harassment doesn't happen. I see it all the time. I'm just saying it doesn't happen as much. In many cases, if a requirement to sleep with the boss was not met, you were fired that day — no severance pay, no nothing. You just did what they said or else. And it didn't matter to these men if you were single or married. There were, however, some bright and cunning women who were able to repeatedly turn down their bosses and still keep their jobs. Too bad these women didn't write a handbook. We could have used it. We still could.

These days, a person would have to be from another planet not to know the sexual-harassment climate of our corporate world. But what about the abusive boss, the one who screams and throws things? What about the nitpicker? Nothing you do is ever up to her standard. You secretly wonder what it would be like to be her spouse or one of her children. Then there is the passive-aggressive boss who tells you that you are doing fine and secretly records every wrong thing you do — only to dump it on you in your yearly review.

More than 80 percent of first-time bosses have not had much supervisory training. Typically, when a manager is considering promoting someone, she will promote the person who exhibits the best work ethic and knows the job better than anyone else. So the company or department loses its best technician and gains a bad manager. She has to do her own work and supervise others as well. As a result of all this stress and new responsibility, the worst in her may come out. Her promotion may not have been a mistake on the company's part; it's obvious that a supervisor has to really know the business. The mistake is made when the company pushes this dutiful employee into the ocean and yells, "SWIM!" without offering swimming lessons.

On the other hand, there are people who were promoted who have no business working in management whatsoever. They weren't even good at the jobs they did before they got promoted. I don't know who they had to schmooze to get their jobs. Even if they had five years of management training, they would still be lousy managers. I'm amazed that some of these people can keep their jobs. Some of them are just flat incompetent.

What about the boss who is a snoop or the boss who expects you to be his slave? And then there is the boss who will write you ugly memos instead of talking with you. Did I mention *your* boss here? Read on, I probably will.

When complaining about our co-workers, part of the problem is that they don't report to us. With bosses, that problem is made worse by the fact that not only do these people not report to us — we report to them. Our paychecks and therefore our livelihoods are dependent on our getting along with our supervisors, and that is often a challenge.

Detestable Bosses

The distasteful personal habits we are so annoyed with in our co-workers are sometimes even worse in our bosses, so we start off once again with disgusting and just plain annoying bosses.

Bad-breath Boss

Dear Jean,

My boss has really bad breath. When he speaks to me, I almost gag. What can I do to let him know of his problem? He is a very defensive person.

Reply:

I know only two options: Get up your courage and tell him, or stay two arms' lengths away. By the way, if you are a coward, there is always www.gentlehints.com.

I have a client who was the person with the bad breath. His secretary kept a bunch of mints in her desk. As he would be walking out of the office for a meeting, she would say, "Wait, here are a couple of mints." It wasn't too long before he asked her if he had a breath problem. She told him the truth, and he was thankful to hear it. She probably saved him a couple of teeth, too. Her courage helped her boss detect early stages of gum disease.

Door-dinging Boss

Dear Jean,

We have assigned parking at work, and I'm very appreciative of this perk, but I have a problem. My parking space is next to that of the president of the company. When she gets out of her car, she always dings my car. Since December, she has put six or seven dents in my car door. Parking spaces are not plentiful downtown. Even if I could find another place, I couldn't afford to pay for it. What do I do?

Reply:

Are you absolutely sure it is your boss who is doing this? Have you seen her do it? This is not a situation in which you should go with your gut feeling. If you are sure about this, you have four options:

1. *Ask if she could be a little more gentle when getting in and out of her car.*
2. *Trade parking places with one of your fellow workers.*
3. *Find another lot, no matter what the cost.*
4. *If you're chicken and don't care about aesthetics, have defensive rubber/plastic stripping applied to the door of your car. That's what boat owners do. Their protectors are called "dock bumpers."*

My Boss Is a Cow

Dear Jean,

The woman who was brought in to be my boss is a cow. Not only is she fat and badly dressed, she also chews gum constantly. What can I do or say that might help her to change her image to fit more easily into our office?

Reply:

Based on what you've said, there is real danger here, and it is not your boss's weight. This attitude you are carrying around can get you into real trouble. My guess is that you've already told several people your feelings, and believe me, sooner or later your boss will know what you are saying about her. I promise.

My hope is that you will learn to see your boss as a competent leader and won't feel compelled to help, teach, or counsel her. That is more along the line of what is expected of her — to help, teach, and counsel you.

Make a list of her assets and read them to yourself every morning. Keep your focus on the positive. Do you best to get rid of the negative pictures and feelings you have about her. If you don't, you're committing career suicide.

If you work very long at all, you will have many bosses you don't like. This is a fact of life. You will get nowhere by holding negative pictures in your mind about your boss. Even if you don't say anything to your co-workers about your boss, your negativity will not only hurt you, it will damage your relationship with your boss, and if found out, maybe your relationship with your next boss, too.

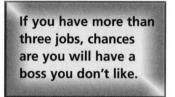

If you have more than three jobs, chances are you will have a boss you don't like.

Boss Is a Chain Smoker

Dear Jean,

I'm a nonsmoker, as are most of my co-workers. Our boss, however, is a chain smoker. I can hardly stand to be in the same room with the woman, yet I must deal with her every day (at close quarters). The smell of her, her office, and our office, to a lesser extent, is enough to choke a horse. I need the job, so what can I do about this smelly situation?

Reply:

Having been a smoker, having worked with smokers, and having lived with a smoker, I can tell you one thing for sure. There is precious little you can do about your boss's sanctioned smoking. You made it clear that you need your job, but do you need that job? You can do one of three things: Accept the smell, take up smoking (which will give you a whole new set of problems), or sniff your way to your next job!

Smoking has become unpopular in business. So if you dislike breathing bad air, don't be shy. When you interview for your next position, be sure to ask if the company has a clean-air policy.

He's Really Moody

Dear Jean,

I have a very moody boss, but I am not moody. I have found that he affects my moods.

What can I do?

Reply:

There is nothing you can do to change your boss's moods. And if you think changing his mood is up to you, you are in for a very tense life. The level of sanity and serenity you have in your life will depend on how well you are able to accept the moodiness of your boss, co-workers, spouse, children, mother-in-law, etc. I'm not suggesting that you learn to like moodiness. You just have to accept it in others.

Acceptance is something you will have to practice. It doesn't come easily. Acceptance doesn't mean you have to like the things people do or say to you. It doesn't mean that you think rude or moody behavior is correct. It just means that you are not willing to act on these behaviors at the moment. You have to get to the point that you understand that someone else's moods say nothing about you. Their moods are not about you. There is very little you can do to lift the spirits of a person who loves to ride an emotional roller coaster.

> **Remember: Your boss's mood is about him, not about you.**

Boss's Blue Words

Dear Jean,

I'm an architect with a small company. My office is between my boss's office and the reception area. My boss occasionally swears and can be heard plainly in the reception area. Some of my best friends are sailors, so I'm no prude, but from an image standpoint, this mortifies me. What can I do?

Reply:

Your boss probably doesn't want to be heard swearing in the reception area any more than you want him to be heard. You can't change your boss's behavior or language. You can, however, ask your boss to swear a little more quietly, or you can shut his office door. Architects should be able to come up with some sound-deadening cork paneling for the boss's office.

Correcting your Boss

In most cases, attempting to modify your boss's habits is a lose-lose battle. Your boss won't change, and you may have to change — jobs.

Correcting the Boss

Dear Jean,

My boss prides herself on being a person who is sophisticated and in the know. For the most part, she is. There is one exception, however. She mis-pronounces several words that she uses quite frequently. I have looked these words up, and I know her pronunciations are incorrect.

She's a lawyer, she's plenty smart, and I know how important it is for her to make it up the ladder. I'm trying to be helpful. She and I are fairly close, so approaching this subject does not make me feel uncomfortable, but I fear that it may embarrass her. Have you any suggestions on how I can help her?

Reply:

Correcting your boss could end up being more embarrassing for you than it is for her. On the other hand, she could enthusiastically thank you. Since you don't know how she will react, why don't you say: "Oh — is that how you pronounce that word? I always thought the emphasis was on the second syllable!"

Privacy Issues

Privacy can be a big issue. If a co-worker goes pawing through our desk, we get pretty angry. When our bosses don't respect our privacy, it adds quite a bit of helplessness, possibly even rage, into the mixture. Does a boss always have a right to intrude on what we consider our personal space at the office? Can he go through my desk? Can she open the mail that is addressed to me and marked "personal"? Where exactly are the boundaries, since I am employed in *his* office?

Nosy Boss

Dear Jean,

Should my boss feel free to dig through my desk whenever she chooses? The woman opens my desk drawers and checks through anything she wishes, whether I'm in the office or not. Can I do something to keep her out of my files and out of my hair? I need my job.

Reply:

It must be very upsetting for you to feel that you have no privacy. In theory, I agree with you. In reality, I can think of several reasons why your boss went through files in your desk:

1. *Your boss was working late or through lunch and needed to find a hard copy of something you had produced.*

2. *Your boss heard that your invoicing was not going out on time and she wanted to make sure it had. (Yes, it would be nice if she would ask you directly.)*

3. *Your boss is the kind of person who wants everything yesterday and was too impatient to wait for you to be at your desk.*

4. *You promised her that you would finish a project at a certain time, but she felt that you wouldn't, so she took back the work she had delegated to you.*

A lot of "hands-on" managers will insist on having their hands on your work as well as their own. It could be that she has a sense of entitlement, thinks there is nothing wrong with going through your files, and will continue to do it as long as you work for her.

As I see it, you only have two choices. You can diplomatically confront your boss or not. It's very important that before you confront your boss, you know beyond a doubt that it is your boss going through your desk and not a co-worker.

Boss Opens My Mail

Dear Jean,

My boss has been opening my mail. The other day after I came back from lunch, there was a stack of mail on my desk, some of it opened, some unopened. Two of the opened pieces were marked "personal." This really threatens my freedom, and I don't like it. I love my job, but I just might quit over this one.

Reply:

Why don't you tell your boss how you feel? I have no idea why your boss is opening your mail. Maybe he or she will tell you. If you really love your job, give your boss a chance to explain. Then the two of you can come to some kind of agreement.

If the idea of bringing up this subject makes your palms sweaty, go down to the local post office and get yourself a mailbox. It will cost a little money, but what is your serenity worth?

If Your Boss Doesn't Respect You

If your bosses don't respect your privacy, you have a serious problem. You need to be able to count on your supervisors' respect, but often that doesn't happen.

Respect relates to more than privacy. A good boss will respect others to the point that she respects herself. My first year in management was pretty revealing.

"She's a jerk," people would say behind my back. And in 1974, I had the reputation of having the most unhappy employees housed under one roof anywhere. I was a perfect example of a very young manager in a high-energy, commission sales environment. I had power, authority, and no grasp of how to treat people. I was disrespectful and demanding. Nobody liked me except my boss.

One thing is for sure, in those early days of my tutelage, my boss didn't like me because I was likable. She liked me because I did what I was hired to do. I made money for the company.

I had favorite sayings such as, "You work, you stay — you don't, you leave," "My way or the highway," and "Don't tell me about the labor pains, show me the baby." General Patton was my hero, and I did everything short of slapping people to motivate them.

Once I had this great idea. I suggested that we hire two new people every month and fire the two lowest producers. My boss said no. My boss and mentor, whom I respected a great deal, was kind enough to let me stick around long enough to learn how to motivate people without terrorizing them.

The thing is, I thought I was being helpful. I acted the way I did because I thought bosses were supposed to *boss*. It seems to me that I might have learned from my mentor's style and treated people like she treated me. Nope. I just couldn't make the connection.

I was committed to success, and because of that I read a series of self-help books. I read anything I could get my hands on that would help me make it in business. When the book *Winning Through Intimidation* came out, my boss suggested that I *not* buy it.

At some point, I learned that motivating people was impossible anyway. The only thing I could do was create a motivational environment in which people would motivate themselves. That's how I do it today.

No Respect

Dear Jean,

I have a problem with my boss. I am coming in to work on time every day; I am working as hard as I can; I am trying to let him see that I take pride in my job, yet I feel that he is showing zero respect for me. What should I do to get some of that respect?

Reply:

Does he treat everyone with disrespect, or is it just you?

If he treats only you this way, there is probably some miscommunication going on here. His picture of what he wants you to do may not be your picture of what you've been doing. Make an appointment to discuss your job with him. Don't tell him ahead of time what you want to speak to him about. If he point-blank asks you, tell the truth. Tell him that the subject you want to discuss is personal.

When you are in front of him, tell him that you would like to feel successful in your job and you don't. Ask him specifically what he wants you to do.

I must point out, however, that some bosses just aren't the accepting type. Some don't give any strokes at all unless you mess up. Another problem is that some bosses refuse to be specific. If that is the case and you can't deal with ambiguity, better take your skills elsewhere.

Boss's Daughter Makes Big Bucks

Dear Jean,

I have been hired recently by a family-owned company. I am the accountant. Recently, the boss's daughter was put on the payroll. She makes more money than I do and she comes to work only a day or two a week. Should I tell my boss how I feel? He will most likely tell me to tend to my own business. What do I do? I think this is ludicrous.

Reply:

One of the hardest things I have ever had to learn is that people do things for their own reasons, not mine! There is little you can do about what your boss pays his daughter.

The way I see it, you have two choices. 1. You can talk to your boss about your feelings. He will probably tell you exactly what you predicted he would say; he'll tell you to "tend to your own business." 2. You can accept the fact that you are going to have to work hard for a living and she is not. Perhaps you can think of her paycheck as her weekly allowance from her dad.

We don't ever have to like things over which we have no control, but for peace of mind, we do have to accept them. Look on the bright side. In a small company, you will have the possibility of making yourself extremely valuable.

Obviously, the company has money, or darling daughter wouldn't be bringing down the big bucks. Keep your nose down, give your new boss 100 percent, and see if you, too, can laugh all the way to the bank.

The best advice I can give a person who is observing a parent-child relationship at work is to stay out of their squabbles. Families are messy and business is complicated. When the two are combined, occasionally the atmosphere will get a little thick.

Parents will typically treat their working children one of two ways. The parents will either be rougher on their children than they are on their employees or they will be easier on their children. Either way, it's not your business. The quickest way to get on the owner's bad list is to get between him and his children — on any issue. So if any family member comes to you and tries to get you to take sides on a particular issue that does not directly affect the way you make a living, keep a low profile.

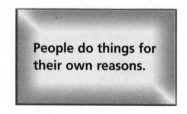

People do things for their own reasons.

Is He a Chauvinist?

Dear Jean,

I work in a large, publicly held company. All in all, I would say it's a pretty good place to work. The chairman of our board is 60 years old and boldly states that he wants women to advance. His actions show that he really does. There is one annoying factor in this scenario. He continues to call women "Honey," "Darlin'," and "Dear." We are getting mixed signals here. What do you think?

Reply:

At first blush, my feeling is that you would do well to cut the guy a little slack. At the risk of reeking of generational chauvinism, you really need to consider the chairman's age. When he was just starting out in his career, the year was about 1955, when many women were wearing dresses and pearls to dust their homes.

The real issue here is: Is he holding women back? Your question indicates that his actions are egalitarian. Hats off to him!

Here is a response to that letter:

Dear Jean,

Why do you think it is OK for a chairman of the board to call people "Honey" and "Darlin'" just because he happens to be of a certain age? If the rules of decency and professionalism apply to me, at 35 years of age, then they apply to everyone in my workplace. I bet I would get in trouble if I went around calling him "Gramps," no matter how capable I believe he is as a person. This chairman of the board should be setting an example by moving women forward, not just as employees in the company, but also in his treatment of women face-to-face as equal professionals.

My reply:

I agree with you. He should change the way he speaks. In all reality, though, he probably won't change. The important thing for you to look at, as someone who answers to him, is the fact that his actions are definitely in line. He is moving women forward in his company. To pester him from below for a few stray words is petty, not productive.

Having come of age during the women's movement, I am unusually sensitive to sexist comments. And I learned early that getting angry got me nowhere. Years ago, I was on the local board of the Institute of Management Accountants. For the first couple of years, I was the only female who regularly attended the meetings.

Every holiday season, we would have "Wives' Night." The board would painstakingly pick a speaker who would appeal to an audience of accountants and nonaccountants, males and females. One November, the topic of the board meeting was Wives' Night. Obviously, there was no awareness of my gender. Maybe they thought of me as one of the guys. They bantered back and forth — "my wife this, and my wife that." After about five minutes, I said, "My wife is really looking forward to this event, but she wants me to ask you what she should wear." My humorous comment brought the house down, and Wives' Night was referred to as Spouses' Night from then on.

None of these men was intentionally sexist. Yes, they were using sexist language, but their intentions were definitely egalitarian. Remember the saying "actions speak louder than words?" They do.

Boss Writes Ugly Memos

Dear Jean,

My boss writes ugly reprimand memos to me. When we see each other, she acts like my best friend. Help! I'm getting mixed messages.

Reply:

It sounds as if you're confused by this behavior, and rightly so. Let me explain how the majority of supervisors and managers get their jobs. They are excellent producers of work; as a matter of fact, they were most likely the best producers in their groups. What happens when the company promotes such a person is that it loses one of its best staff members and pos-

sibly gets a mediocre or poor manager. Your boss is probably one of those people who may be competent and yet unequipped to be a manager. It's obvious by these memos that your boss is trying to tell you something and does not feel comfortable talking about the problem in person.

This is a sticky situation, and I think it would serve you well to try to talk about this to her face-to-face. You must have the courage to do this, or you may never find out exactly what you are doing that is objectionable. Unless you know what it is, you can't change it.

Pick up the last ugly memo, ask for an appointment with your boss, then tell her that you want to please her. Ask what specifically is not satisfactory. Listen carefully, then correct the way you handled that task or situation in the past.

If you receive still another ugly memo, ask if you can meet with her for 10 or 15 minutes every week so you two can cover issues such as this. Remember to thank her for this feedback. The clearer the communication regarding your performance, the faster you will progress with her and your company.

Public Disrespect

Bosses aren't exactly required to respect their employees. It probably isn't written into their job description; it's just one of the things that differentiates a good boss from a bad boss. This requirement crosses an important line, however, if the disrespect becomes public.

Public Put-down

Dear Jean,

I work as a teller at a bank. A couple of weeks ago, we had a computer problem and I made a mistake on a customer's account. We fixed it, but yesterday my branch manager was on the phone at my teller station talk-

ing to someone about my mistake. Instead of just saying a teller made a mistake, she was using my name and specific amounts.

It made me feel really uncomfortable in front of the customers. I think this was unprofessional. I feel rotten already, and this is like adding insult to injury. Do I need to talk to her about it, or do I need to call my district manager? What should I do?

Reply:

I think the best thing to do is to talk to her about it before you call the district manager. She may not have been aware of how insensitive she was and how this made you feel.

She may not have intended to put you down. The only thing you can do is make an appointment to talk to her privately. Tell her that what she said in public felt like a put-down to you. Look her straight in the eye and say, "Did you mean it that way?" Talk it out. If you don't like the way your meeting turns out, then call the district manager.

Boss Is a Put-down Artist

Dear Jean,

I'm the vice president of engineering for a $50 million company. My boss has a habit of making sarcastic remarks to me in front of my subordinates. I'm not the only one he terrorizes — I've seen this happen to several other people at my level. I'm 10 years away from retirement, so it's not wise for me to make waves, but sometimes I want to deck him.

This problem is really getting to me, and I'm tired of spending so much money on ulcer medication, not to mention the resentment I'm building up. What would you do if you were in my place?

Reply:

Most everyone will agree that a sarcastic boss is toxic. The suggestion I'm about to make will take a lot of courage. Your boss sounds as though he may be a bit stubborn and unreasonable. He is getting some payoff out of this behavior. Maybe he is insecure and he needs to act this way to feel important.

If it were causing him a real problem, he would stop. Because being sarcastic pumps him up, there is very little you can do. There is something you can try, but you will need to wait for the right time and the right circumstances.

It's best to make an appointment with him. If that is not possible, wait until you have your boss's full attention. Tell him exactly how you feel. A word of caution — make sure you are fully composed. Any sign of anger will start an argument. Say something such as, "When you make insulting comments to me in front of other people, I feel as though I am 12 years old. Even though you may have good intentions, it's demotivational to me. If I do something that you don't agree with, I'm certainly willing to listen to your point of view. Would you be willing to reprimand me behind closed doors?"

Then, by all means, be silent. Even if it takes a full minute for him to respond, maintain eye contact. If he is reasonable, he is likely to respond in a positive manner. If he is not, and you are unwilling to polish up your resume, then walk on eggshells and call the pharmacy to see if you can order Tagamet by the case.

Here's another way to handle sarcastic remarks: Just look straight into the offender's eyes and say, "Oooh, that sounded like an insult. Did you mean it that way?" This is a benign-sounding little comment, but said at the right time and in the right place, it's powerful.

> **No one can make you feel bad about yourself without your permission.**

James Redfield says in the *Celestine Prophecy*, "Each of us seeks to remain on top in an encounter. If we succeed in outwitting the other person and our viewpoint prevails, then we feel strong rather than weak and we receive a psychological boost." There are people — and many of them are bosses — who wake up every morning wondering whom they can tear into (incidentally, the word *sarcastic* comes from the Greek language and means "to tear flesh").

You see these attackers everywhere. Some of these people are in supervisory management. A few are in upper management. These people are negative, critical, demanding, hostile, and insecure. They want to increase *their* energy, so they steal some. Those subtle put-downs are their way of stealing energy from you. When you feel worse, they feel better. Insulting *you* fills *them* with energy.

Most people cannot successfully work for these types of bosses. Some can, though; I've seen them. The ones who can let those negative comments roll like water off a duck's back. I'm not one of those people. An occasional insult doesn't bother me much, but a constant, steady flow of insults and sniping depletes me. As a result, my resistance gets low and my physical health suffers.

If you find that your sleeping habits have changed, you have more headaches than usual, or you get colds more often, you may be suffering from "toxic boss syndrome" (there is a "toxic co-worker syndrome," too). In other words, if your body's talking to you — listen.

Talking about Your Boss

Your boss may not be the best in the world. For the sake of argument, let's say she borders on being abusive. No matter what she says about you or to you, do not talk about her behind her back. Not only does that bring you down to her level, it just doesn't work. This is critically important, whether you are staying in your current position or leaving for a better one.

Never Bad-mouth the Boss

Dear Jean,

My former boss is nothing short of abusive. That's why I left my last job.

When people ask me to explain why I left my last position, what should I say about this jerk of a boss?

Reply:

In a monthly column in the business magazine Management Account-ing, *Robert Half of Robert Half International addressed this very situation. "Heath" had six years at a manufacturing company. When his boss left the company, a really disagreeable man took over. Heath did not see eye to eye with his new boss from day one, so he quit.*

In Heath's letter of resignation, he made negative comments about his former boss. Little did he know that the man who made him a job offer was a golfing buddy of his old boss.

His old boss naturally had a few unflattering things to say about Heath and his lack of courtesy when resigning. Things didn't turn out so well. Heath was called and told that because of last-minute budgetary changes, his new offer was being withdrawn.

Robert Half's advice: No matter what your previous boss was like, avoid the urge to say anything negative about him or her. My advice: No matter what your previous boss was like, avoid the urge to say anything negative about him or her — ever.

Don't Go Along with Bad-mouthing the Boss

Dear Jean,

What do I do about the fact that my boss's supervisor keeps talking to me about the inadequacies of my boss and what a bad job he's doing? I think this person is right about my boss, but how do I handle this?

Reply:

It doesn't matter if your boss's supervisor is right or not. It's not your business. This is a political Pandora's box for you. Get out of this triangulation right away. If you really feel that your boss is incompetent, make plans to look for another position. Until you do, avoid saying anything bad about your boss to anyone. As soon as you can find the courage, tell your boss's boss that these conversations make you feel uncomfortable.

My Boss Bad-mouths Me

Dear Jean,

My boss is talking about my work behind my back. I know this to be true because two people came to me separately and told me the things he had said. The stories were identical. I like my job. I used to like my boss a lot, too. What do I do?

Reply:

This is sticky, because it is difficult to confront him without revealing your sources. First, go to the people who told you what he said and ask them how they feel about you confronting him. Assure them you will not divulge their names. Because there are two people who have heard these stories, he will not know exactly who carried the information to you.

Then make an appointment to talk with your boss privately. Explain to him that you love your job and that you desire an open line of communication. Tell him what you have heard, and ask if he will come directly to you if he has a complaint about your work. Be sure to let him know you are open to suggestions about how you can improve your work.

This is not a three-strikes-you're-out game. If you hear that he has not stopped blabbing, let me suggest some action. Bring your resume up to date and prepare for a job search.

That's Not My Job

Have you ever had a supervisor ask you to do something that you didn't want to do? So has everybody else. Many times, this gives you the opportunity, however irritating, to expand your abilities. You may learn something or even improve your position because of it.

The question is, what is the difference between having to do something you don't want to do, that you don't feel is part of your job description, and doing something you shouldn't do, just because it was your supervisor who asked you? What do you do if you decide that what your boss is asking you to do crosses the line into something you won't do?

Not in My Job Description

Dear Jean,

I was hired as an assistant manager. As the months progress, the manager seems to be taking advantage of my hard work and asking me to do quite a few additional tasks that are not in my job description. I feel I should be getting paid a lot more than I am because of this. Do I have grounds to ask for a raise or am I stuck with what I agreed to as wages until my yearly review? There is no opportunity to advance until the manager leaves or until the business has substantial growth.

Reply:

If I had a nickel for every time I have heard this question, I would be drinking café latté in Paris. You can ask for a raise any time. Just be prepared for the response. It could be, "No."

There is the possibility that you are being used. There is also the possibility that you are being given a big opportunity. I wonder which it is?

I'd like to share a story about an experience of mine before I opened my business. I was in my mid-20s and working for a woman who had been accepted to the Program for Management Development at Harvard Business School. I was given total responsibility for keeping the business open — and profitable. I was paid a small sum each month for doing so, and I felt it was not nearly enough for such "do-or-die" responsibility.

One particularly stressful day, I had had it. I sought the counsel of a trusted friend who had been in the business world a lot longer than I.

I unloaded for about 30 minutes. Calmly, he said, "Jean, how much would *you pay to learn how to run a business all by yourself?" Not having a clue where he was going with this, I thought about it and answered, "$10,000." He was silent for a moment and then he said, "Isn't this something! You're getting paid to do it!"*

I'm still amazed by the statement, "It's not in my job description." The business would grind to a screeching halt if every office employee stayed within a tightly defined job description. What ever happened to initiative?

Pretend for a moment that you are a temporary and you and your child are living from paycheck to paycheck. Imagine that it's payday, you receive your check, and it is for the wrong amount. You've been shorted $75 and your rent is four days late. You call the temp service, and the person who usually handles payroll matters has been hospitalized. How would you feel if the person who took your call would say, "I'm sorry, you'll have to wait till Marsha gets back. This is not in my job description"?

Bill Paying Is Not My Job

Dear Jean,

I'm required at my job to pay my boss's household bills. How can I tell him politely that this is not part of my job?

Reply:

My husband disagrees with my advice to you on this question. He had 22 years at a large corporation. In his experience, having someone in your department pay your personal bills was strictly taboo. But here is my opinion: If your boss asked you to do it, and it's not immoral, illegal, or against written policy, it is part of your job.

I am assuming that your boss is an executive or owns the company you work for. Even if he's not, if I were you, I would take out my pen, smile, and be appreciative for a fair paycheck and a nice place to work.

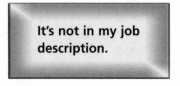

It's not in my job description.

After all, what's another 15 minutes a week? As my assistant, Susan, says, "It all pays the same."

I Don't Do Coffee

Dear Jean,

I'm not a secretary, and I don't do coffee. Here's the problem. My boss wants me to make coffee every morning so I can offer it to my clients when they come in for consultations. "More homelike," he says. Guess who gets to clean the pot at the end of the day? What should I tell my boss, one man to another? Thanks.

Reply:

I can't tell by your question if you're miffed because he asked you to do work that you feel is beneath you or if you have a philosophical disagreement with creating a homelike atmosphere at the office.

Personally, I think the coffee idea is a good one. The more comfortable your clients feel, the longer they will want to stay. The longer they stay, the more time you will have to conduct business on your own turf.

When I have had similar dilemmas in the past, a colleague of mine put it this way: "Jean, do you wanna line your ego or your pockets?"

Relief Receptionist Resentment

Dear Jean,

My boss is asking me to be "relief receptionist." My real job is administrative assistant. Don't you think he is being unfair to expect me to be a receptionist when our real receptionist goes out to lunch?

Reply:

We have a similar situation in our office. I require that someone be at our front desk eight hours a day. Although I feel uncomfortable pulling my administrative assistant away from her work, my commitment to our clients outweighs my regret.

There will always be things in our work life we don't like and don't want to do. Try to keep a willing attitude about this and other office inconveniences. I doubt if your boss regards this as punishment. I hope you won't either.

Here is a response I received:

Dear Jean,

I understand where you are coming from when you say that the administrative assistant should be willing to answer phones as a relief. I also understand where she is coming from, though. Being in the same type of position myself, I feel that I worked very hard to move myself off the phones. My job has grown in complication and responsibility, and I am ready to do something other than answer phones with my work time. One of the troubles I am worried about in a similar vein is that if the receptionist is sick or, even worse, leaves without notice, I am the obvious default, and there I am on the phones again. Is it really possible to get away from the phones?

Reply:

Who is on the other end of the line? A customer? The important thing is that answering phones is not a bad thing, a punishment, or a demotion. It doesn't change who you are or what you do. What it does show is that you are willing to help the company when needed, and for most bosses, that is more precious than gold.

We have a young woman in our office who is willing to do anything for the good of the company. She was 23 and right out of college when she started to work for us.

She started at the front desk. She is 26 now, has advanced into a project manager for us, and has nearly doubled her salary. Why did she promote so fast? Because she is willing to do the little things that no one else jumps at.

Her primary job is to provide technical services in relationship

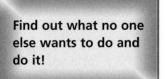

Find out what no one else wants to do and do it!

to our computer network and database. But she will put together office furniture, install doorbells (buying the components at the hardware store), curl ribbons for client gifts, and run errands in the rain. She will also fill in for anyone who is out of the office. This is the stuff that promotions and raises are made of.

Lazy Supervisor

Dear Jean,

The person who has been named my supervisor is coming in late and leaving early. Our superiors seem to know this is happening. Our new supervisor will not do the work she is being paid to do. She expects the other employees to do her work because she is now the supervisor. Should I go to someone above, or should I leave it alone, since management knows about her behavior and has not done anything? This has made it hard for the rest of us to do our job.

Reply:

Maybe the higher-ups do know. Maybe the higher-ups don't know. Maybe she was promoted because she was a "boss's pet." Maybe she is already on probation. Maybe she'll get fired next week. Maybe you will.

What I am trying to say is that as much as we want to know all the answers, we don't. There will always be information that is not available to us. And because you are not 100 percent sure what is going on with your supervisor and her bosses, it is best for you to keep your mind on your work and pick up her slack if you can. Unless you have proof that she is breaking the law or is into some dark activity that will jeopardize the company, your complaints will be classified as whining or complaining.

Caution: She is your new boss. It is your job to make her look good. If in a couple of months you still feel as you do today, it's OK to reevaluate the situation. If at that time you still have a beef with her, go to her, not to her boss.

More Scut Work

Dear Jean,

I was the last person hired in my department, so that means I get a lot of scut work sent my way — like now I have to plan the company picnic for August, and I've never even been to one. Is that fair, Jean?

Reply:

Well…you'll get to go to a company picnic now!

Author and public speaker Brian Tracy talks about this in his video presentation, "Pathways toward Personal Progress," which is part of his Effective Manager Seminar Series. He says that to get ahead, we must separate ourselves from the pack in these ways:

> **Whenever you point a finger, remember there are three fingers pointing back at you.**

- *Always be working on the tasks your boss considers most important.*
- *Always do more than you are paid for.*
- *Be willing to do "dog work."*
- *Volunteer for jobs that nobody else wants.*

There are many other ways to do this, but these are my favorites. The best advice I can give you is to thank your boss for the scut work. This is an excellent opportunity to be noticed by the higher-ups.

Make a commitment to put together the best picnic ever. You won't be sorry.

Pack My Things?

Dear Jean,

Our company is moving to another location. The company has asked each of us to spend half of a workday packing up stuff from our own cubicles and loading it into our personal vehicles for next-day delivery. Does that sound fair to you, Jean? Should I refuse to do the movers' job?

Reply:

If I'm understanding you correctly, your company is willing to pay you your regular pay to pack your cubicle. Lighten up. Look at the bright side. At the very least, you will know where everything is.

Not everyone agrees:

Dear Jean,

I felt that your reply about the person who was required to pack up her cubicle was out of line. You addressed a real problem as though it were nothing. What if her vehicle isn't big enough to carry the things from her cubicle? Are some of the things she will be transporting company property such as computers or files? Will she be liable if any items are stolen or damaged in transit? What if she hurts herself carrying heavy boxes she has no business carrying? There are some very real concerns here. I know you didn't have much information, but you could have treated her problem a little more seriously.

Reply:

If this is the case, you are right. Moving big boxes and heavy computers is out of the question. I am assuming she is packing only her personal items. If this is the case, I think it is generous of the company not to send movers to go through her personal items, pack them, and maybe even break them. This way, she knows exactly where all of her stuff is and what kind of condition she will find it in when she reports to the new location the next day.

Bosses and Their Whims

What if your boss expects you to drop what you are doing and tend to her every time she has a whim?

Boss-imposed Time

Dear Jean,

My boss is constantly appearing in my office wanting to talk about projects we are working on in our department. I don't have time for these intrusions. How do I ask my boss to stop this?

Reply:

You seem like a very responsible person. It sounds like lengthy discussions are annoying to you and you would rather work than talk; however, this is your boss and your boss is, in essence, your customer. In other words, the person you need to please most is the person you

> **A big part of your job is to make your boss look good. If you don't believe it, make her look bad.**

report to. There is no way to completely eliminate boss-imposed time, but you can cut down on the interruptions.

Ask if the two of you can meet privately when you can have the full attention of your supervisor. When you meet, propose a "work in progress" report. This can be a weekly or daily written or verbal report, depending on how your boss likes to receive information. This will be a win-win situation. You will be producing much-needed information for your boss on a regular basis, which automatically gives you more uninterrupted work time.

Boss-imposed time can be frustrating, and it's true that many supervisors and managers think whatever is pressing on *them* should be of utmost importance to *you*. This is true if you have only one boss. It gets complicated when you report to five people and they all think their pet projects should be on your front burner. Or worse yet, they are miffed at you because their projects weren't done yesterday. If you've talked with them to find out which project was really the most important and all they did was fight, you still don't know what to do next. If you find yourself in a pickle like this, look at all your projects and rate them in order of profit making or cost saving.

Your priorities will become clearer. Anything with the potential of making a profit or losing money within the next few weeks goes first, and everything else follows behind. Generally speaking, a proposal is more important than filing (no matter how big the stack is). An invoice is more important than shopping around for a new copier. Designing a sales letter is more important than reconciling the bank account.

> **You must learn to be a good time manager if you want to advance.**

Good time-management and prioritizing skills are a must if you want to get along with everyone in your office and if you want to advance. Invest in a good time-management program. There are several popular courses. Head for the Web and look up "time management."

I'm Not His Personal Handmaiden

Dear Jean,

I work in a large retail store. When the district manager comes, he expects me to do my regular work, but he also expects me to follow him like his personal handmaiden. He even asked me to get his awful sports coat from the cleaners. What do you suggest I do?

Reply:

You could say: "Look, Bubba, I didn't spend four years in college to pick up after you. My major was advertising, not gofering. You are stealing from the company when you indiscriminately waste my time by engaging me in nonprofit-making activities. You're my boss and you're supposed to have better judgment than I do, but you don't. How did you get your degree, by mail order?"

On the other hand, if you have a lot of bills or a family to support, you may want to look for a more refined way of expressing yourself.

Even though your boss is asking you to do some things that you find distasteful, I see three options. 1. Confront him. 2. Do what he asks and don't complain. 3. Take your talent elsewhere.

Confronting him probably won't work. Somewhere in his value system, he can easily justify asking you to do things that might be incongruous with today's work climate. It's doubtful that he will change unless his boss asks him to do so.

If you continue to grant his unusual requests and feel angry or indignant as a result, you will build up resentment against him. This is dangerous because one of these days you will blow up. And when you do, you can bet it will be at an inopportune time.

If you love your job and make a salary that you feel is commensurate with the work you do, you may want to put up with your district manager's awful sports coat and strange idiosyncrasies.

By the same token, if his behavior crosses your value system and you just can't get over it, plan your escape!

Don't get me wrong. I don't think doing personal errands for the boss should be acceptable as an everyday occurrence. As a matter of fact, in some cases it might be regarded as personally offensive. I'm just asking you to weigh the pros and cons.

Holiday Shopping for Boss's Mom

Dear Jean,

Christmas is coming and I'm dreading it — not because of all the things I have to do at home. I'm dreading it because of my boss's mother-in-law. Every year in mid-December, she shows up at the office for the same thing — my help.

My boss hands me a list and asks me to take care of Mother Stone's Christmas shopping — that very afternoon. Five years of this drill is enough. My boss's boss even knows about this and says nothing. What do you suggest?

Reply:

In answering your letter, I'm assuming that this particular type of boss-imposed time is the exception and not the rule. However, the fact that your boss's boss knows about this request makes me think that this behavior is generally accepted at the company where you work. The way I see it, there are several ways you can approach your boss. Here are some possible solutions:

Solution Number One: Get up your nerve and make a "formal" appointment with your boss. Tell her that the time you spend on Mother Stone's Christmas list might be better spent by your doing special projects inside the office, and ask if there might be someone else who could do the shopping (possibly someone who has been at the company less time than you). Be straightforward, low key, and direct. The worst thing that can happen is that your boss can emphatically say NO!

Solution Number Two: You could put on a happy face, head for the mall, and whittle down — with your boss's knowledge — some of your own Christmas list while you are buying for Mother Stone. I've worked with several people who would love to go to the mall on company time. You might enjoy it yourself.

Solution Number Three: You can stomp your feet, make a hateful face, and yell in a screeching tone, "That's not in my job description! I didn't come to work here to be Santa's helper!"

A word of caution: I can almost guarantee that if you choose Solution Number Three, you won't be shopping for Mother Stone this year — or any year thereafter. You may want to take this yearly request as a very special compliment to you. Both boss and mother-in-law bow to your taste.

Learn Spanish and Like It

Dear Jean,

My boss wants all of us to learn Spanish. I thought my days of struggling with this kind of stuff were over. He's asked us to enroll in a class on our own time in the evenings. Are we required to do this? I like my job, but I resent having to learn a foreign language to keep it.

Reply:

You really need to call an attorney who specializes in employment to answer this question. My guess is that your employer can't dictate what you do on your own time.

Let's address your feelings about this issue. As far as your days of "struggling with this stuff" being over, probably not. As long as you continue to work, you will undoubtedly be inconvenienced by the wishes and dictates of other people. A helpful axiom: "Grant me the serenity to accept the things I cannot change, the courage to change the things I can, and the wisdom to know the difference."

Knowing Spanish will make you a much more valuable employee in the workplace. Have you thought of that?

Recently, I read an article about how quickly the job market is changing. The article said that people who are now graduating from high school will have seven different careers in their lifetime. That indicates to me that you should never quit learning. School is never over for the pro.

I Gave at the Office

Dear Jean,

The senior partner in our firm has a real problem with me. He is adamant that I should contribute to charity or spend time working in the community. Granted, I can afford to do one or the other, but I don't want to. I have many things in my life that I want to do with my money and time. What do you think?

Reply:

If you want me to agree, you asked the wrong person. Cavett Robert, a mentor of mine, once said, "Service is the only rent

> **Service is the only rent we pay to occupy our space on the planet.**

you pay to occupy your space on the planet." Even though I respect your opinion and your right to privacy, I think social responsibility is an important part of leadership. Whether it's at your church, your neighborhood association, or a not-for-profit organization, your talents are desperately needed in the community.

Although I'm not sure your boss has the absolute power over your after-work endeavors, he does have his opinions, and your upward mobility may depend on them.

Here is a response I received:

Dear Jean,

On principle, I agree with you. Everyone should contribute somehow to the community. I know that I do. This is not something that can be forced, though. It is not right for an employer to force his employees to use their personal time or money for charity purposes. This is the kind of gift that can come only from the heart, not from the boss's orders.

Reply:

You are absolutely right. Social responsibility cannot be forced, but it can be suggested and even emulated. I hope this person takes this suggestion to heart and starts to give something back to his community.

It May Not Be Legal

Some people were taught early on never to disagree with their boss and to always do what the boss says. You may have been taught that the boss is always right and that you should not argue or question the authority of your employer. Just because your boss is asking you to do something, it doesn't mean that it is right. It may not even be legal.

Boss Tells Pregnant Woman to Stay out of Sight

Dear Jean,

I'm pregnant and really beginning to show. I'll probably look as big as a house in a couple of months because I'm carrying twins. My boss hinted that he would prefer that I confine myself to the "back office" where customers never come. I feel a little self-conscious, but I think it is because of the way he acts. What should I do? My husband has been out of work for three months. We already have two children, so I need this job.

Reply:

Recently, I was watching an old movie. It was made in the '40s. The lead actress was pregnant (expecting, as they called it in polite company). At no time did the camera show a full shot of her. It was as if there was something unclean and embarrassing about a woman having a baby. I was disgusted by what I saw on that film. I had a similar feeling when I read your letter.

You tell me that your boss "hinted" that he wants you to stay out of the public eye? The best thing to do is ask him specifically what he means by this hinting. If your boss does in fact want you to hide out for several months, he is sending you a very strong signal.

To me, this is certainly unacceptable behavior on his part. Aside from this being just plain insensitive, it is legally questionable. The EEOC will love hearing about this.

The fact that you really need your job will make this an agonizing decision for you and your husband. I can't make this decision for you. But I strongly suggest that if you do decide to wait this out, keep your eye on the want ads. This is probably not the best place to spend the next 10 years.

Family Imposition

Dear Jean,

I work at a large, family-owned business. I'm the receptionist. The founder has turned over the day-to-day operations to his son. Any time anyone in the family leaves town for the weekend, the phones get transferred to my house. Then I have to sit at home answering the phones. I don't get paid for this and I have four small children, so I'm dreadfully busy on weekends. How can I address this with the family members?

Reply:

With your four children, I'm sure you don't want to jeopardize your position. Even though the federal Wage and Hour Department might be able to help you solve your problem, contacting it will give you a whole new set of problems.

On the other side of the coin, as annoying as this situation is, I'm sure the family you work for trusts you a great deal or they wouldn't leave you with this level of responsibility.

What to do? Go to your direct supervisor and ask if you could share this responsibility with someone in the office. Another option would be to ask to be paid for the time you work out of the office or to see if they would consider hiring an after-hours emergency answering service. Cheerfully explain that you would like to have a life, and having freedom on the weekend is part of that life. If they are not cooperative, you can report them to Wage and Hour and risk your boss's irritation, quit your job, or accept the imposition and never mention it again.

Many people who impose on you are not trying to do harm to you. They are thinking about what they want. They are self-centered. Sometimes when you explain how their requests affect your life, they will say something like, "Oh, I never thought of that. Sure, we can make an adjustment."

Only a Dummy Would Dummy up Expense Reports

Dear Jean,

I work for a large oil and gas firm. My boss asks me to "dummy up" his expense reports so he can be reimbursed for expenses that I am sure *(because he told me) he has not incurred. I am not talking about $100 here and $100 there. Over a year's time, this adds up to a couple of months of my salary. This makes me feel very uncomfortable. What should I do?*

Reply:

This is serious, and there is a good chance that at some time you will be caught in the cross fire. Sooner or later, someone will find out. You may even be courting legal problems for yourself.

In most companies, the behavior of your boss is called theft. Does your company provide a way for you to alert upper management and still remain anonymous?

Maybe you'd better update your resume.

Quitting your job sometimes results in a bigger problem than you had in the first place. If you can work out your problems without changing jobs, do it. You'll be better off in the long run. There is no way to know if a new job is better than the one you already have. Just as your job in an interview is to sell yourself, the interviewer's job is to sell you. As good as you think you are at sizing up people, believe me, you can be fooled.

There are several legitimate reasons to quit your job, however. If you are asked to lie, if your boss is breaking the law, or if you are being physically, sexually, or mentally abused, you need to find a new place to work.

Make My Child Work, Too?

Dear Jean,

Recently I had to miss a Friday because of an illness. I offered to make up the work over the weekend. My personnel director then told me to take my 11-year-old daughter with me on Saturday, put a uniform on her, and put her to work. I did not take my daughter to work, but I am afraid that I will get fired. I am having a really hard time dealing with this. I don't know whether to quit my job or to go to the owners of the company and tell them. I really need some advice on this.

Reply:

You did the right thing by not putting a uniform on your daughter and taking her to work the shift with you. Ordinarily, I would encourage you to work this out with the person who gave you the directive, especially if the person is your direct supervisor. This case is different. This incident needs to be reported.

> **Just because your boss is asking you to do something doesn't mean it is right. It may not even be legal.**

In my 20-plus years in business, I have never heard such an outrageous request. I'm shrugging my shoulders. Your personnel director is either exceptionally uninformed or just plain dumb. Scary! If you can manage to look for another job, do it.

Dealing with More Than One Supervisor

Dealing with just one poor supervisor is hard enough. Dealing with more than one is even more difficult. One supervisor tells you one thing to do, and the other tells you another thing to do. Pretty soon you don't know which thing to do. Don't pull your hair out. There is a solution — read on.

Conflicting Directions

Dear Jean,

I am in a position where I have direct input from the owner of the company. Often, after the owner gives me directions, my direct supervisor later tells me something totally opposite from what the owner tells me to do. What should I do?

Reply:

These two people need to get together. When your supervisor tells you something, just say, "The owner told me to do this, you're telling me to do this, let's get together and find out what I am really supposed to do." Theoretically, your direct supervisor is the one who tells you what to do, but the owner of the company is the one who signs the checks. That puts you in a sticky situation. Once those two get together, talk about it, and come to an agreement, you will be more comfortable in your job.

When I was young, I worked at a nursing home. The head nurse made certain requests of me and the owner made different requests. It didn't take long to tell where the real power was. The power player was the head nurse. She followed up on whatever she asked me to do. The owner would forget what he asked me to do. So even though the owner signed the checks, the nurse had the most operational power. By the way, the *owner* even did what the head nurse asked him to do.

Paralegals Drunk with Power

Dear Jean,

I work at a medium-sized law firm. The attorney I work for is a demanding but fair person. That's not my problem. The paralegals who work for our firm are drunk with power. Not one of them has had any management experience prior to coming here. They bully everyone around without regard to esprit de corps. They have no manners.

There is one in particular who has it in for me. She is just plain hostile and "in my face" every time I turn around. I technically don't report to her, but I am responsible for doing work for her.

At our firm, personnel grievances are to be made to the office administrator. Should I complain? He knows about this situation and has done nothing to help.

Reply:

Unfortunately, there are many people in the workforce who have no management savvy. It's too bad they are in management, but that's just the way it is.

Office administrators on the whole would rather hear about solutions than problems. Before you make a formal plea to the administrator, make sure you have done everything you can do to remedy this distasteful situation.

Here's a quick and easy formula to use in a confrontation. This works as well with your family as it does at work. You only have to remember three things: I feel _____ when you _____. Please _____.

After the words "I feel," select a word that really describes the way this treatment makes you feel. Then after the words "when you," describe the behavior you find objectionable. And finally, after the word "please," explain what you would like to have happen.

I'm simplifying in the interest of space. Even so, here's how it may sound: "I feel demotivated when you toss things on my desk and yell, because I do the best I can every day. Please sit down with me when you have a request. I'll be happy to respond."

Caution! You must remain calm. The calmer you are, the more impact this will have. Practice this and role-play with a friend until you can say the words without any anger in your voice.

Should You Have to Change?

One of my first bosses was also a great mentor of mine. She was watching the way I dealt with the people under my supervision, and she noticed (with no trouble, I assure you) that I had no tact. I expected my employees to march along doing their jobs with no positive feedback from me. The trouble was, my boss expected me to fix *myself*. Was that a fair request?

In his book, *Stairway to Success*, Nido Qubein asks, "When you decide to buy new furniture for your home, what do you have to do?" He answers with, "You probably have to get rid of most of your old furniture. The same thing holds true of old ideas and old ways. You have to let go of old ideas and habits you've grown comfortable with." That is exactly what I had to do.

Change My Personality?

Dear Jean,

My boss would like me to be more of a people person. Because I supervise five people, this has come up on every review. It's not that I don't like people, but I find many people extremely annoying. How can I change my personality?

Reply:

I don't think it's a good idea to try to change your personality. It sounds like all you need to do is add some people skills, and believe me, they can be acquired. The best training for this in the nation is the Dale Carnegie course. I have seen a 10-week course dramatically alter a person's career opportunities. These skills are critical. You will learn things such as how to be a good listener and how to get others to talk about themselves; how to show genuine interest in other people; how to supervise without criticizing, condemning, or complaining; and how just smiling can make people around you feel differently. As a bonus, Dale Carnegie training (at www.dalecarnegie.com) will enhance your family relationships as well.

Just like the person in this question, I had to change the way I dealt with people. To do this, I listened to educational tapes night and day. I listened to them when I got ready for work; I listened to them as I drove to work.

This became a lifelong habit, and even though the subject matter of the tapes I listen to changes, I always take along six to 12 hours of listening on any road trip. Head for the public library. See what it has. My largest source of business education tapes is Nightingale Conant. You can find them on the Web at www.nightingale.com.

Make it a goal to turn on a tape the minute you get in the car.

Before too long, you will have an education equivalent to a master's degree just from the time you have spent in the car.

Too Opinionated

Dear Jean,

I work for a company that tells me I am too opinionated. How can I change that about myself?

Reply:

I've never known an opinionated person who stopped being opinionated. I don't believe that a total personality change is likely for you or for anyone else. You can, however, learn to keep yourself from responding to things if you think your response might hurt or offend someone. I'm suggesting that when something comes up that gets you upset, just be silent. By being silent, you will appear more tolerant and less opinionated.

Because it is very difficult to measure your own results in this area, share your dilemma with a trusted friend. The personality trait that you describe as "opinionated" will show itself in a friendship before it will in a work situation. We are more comfortable with our friends; therefore, we are less guarded. That being the case, ask your friend to monitor your progress.

Do tell your friend your goal, but don't tell your friend your strategy of keeping quiet. In a couple of weeks, ask your friend if you seem to be less opinionated as a whole.

There is a book that can help you in your quest to have a more pleasing personality — How to Win Friends and Influence People, by Dale Carnegie. It is by far the best book available on relationships, on and off the job.

Another solution — go into business for yourself. Make your opinions pay off.

Catch Them Doing Something Right

Dear Jean,

On my last performance appraisal, my boss told me I need to give recognition to my staff. I explained that my staff members know perfectly well when they are not up to par. I don't feel the need to get all mushy and give people standing ovations for doing their jobs. My boss thinks differently, and I can tell you right now that frothy emotional displays are not for me. How can I do what my boss wants and not compromise my values?

Reply:

You will have to compromise a little. In the classic, popular book The One Minute Manager, *we learn to catch people doing things right and praise them for it. I will adapt that concept to fit your style. Catch one of your employees doing something above and beyond the call of duty. Describe the performance or behavior you are recognizing and be clear on why you are recognizing it. Express your appreciation and then say thank you. That's all there is to it.*

This will be hard for you at first. Most likely you and your boss have a different idea about what constitutes "above and beyond the call of duty." Be sure to discuss this with him so both of you are in agreement as to which kinds of behaviors you want to recognize.

Remember — the performance that you praise is the performance that will be repeated.

What if your boss catches you doing something wrong? There is only one good piece of advice in that situation.

Caught with the Company Car

Dear Jean,

Our company furnishes a car for my job. It is for business use only. Last Friday night, I took my family to a movie. Guess who was parked next to my family and me and the company car? Yep. It was the VP in charge of my division. He didn't speak to me. What should I do?

Reply:

My advice to you is to "'fess up fast."

To some corporations, using the company car for personal use is similar to taking home the company VCR to tape the Super Bowl. I'm sure this situation is uncomfortable for you and you wish it would just go away. It won't.

The only thing you can do is to tell your direct supervisor what you did. What happens to you from that point on is out of your hands.

About that division VP — it would be a good idea to apologize to him. Even if he didn't notice you, he will remember you for your willingness to correct your behavior. And from now on, leave the company car at home.

Just for fun, call 10 people tonight and ask them what they think of their bosses. My hunch is two or three will have mostly nice things to say about their bosses. The rest will give you a zillion reasons why they think they are smarter than their bosses and why their bosses are incompetent, insensitive jerks.

Over the years, I've heard thousands of bad-boss stories. My favorite was told to me by a woman named Joy who worked for the owner of an insurance agency. Outside the agency, Butch was known as both vigorous and resourceful. To his employees, he was known as Jekyl and Hyde. He had temper tantrums, and no one knew what

> **For *things* to change, *you've* gotta change.**

exactly would bring them on. People walked on eggshells every day. Even people who had worked for him for several years could not figure out what to expect from him from day to day.

You might be wondering why anyone would work for a man like that. Money, mostly. He paid more than any of his competitors. And as Joy said, "He is quite pleasant between eruptions."

Butch owned the office building where he and his employees worked. The housekeeping service came in only on Saturdays, so it was important to Butch that the offices were kept clean by his employees during the week.

One day Butch came in at about 7:00 A.M. to find that the salespeople had worked late the night before and had forgotten to put their plates and glasses into the dishwasher. He went into a rage. He took every wastebasket from beside the desks and poured the trash on top and into the drawers of the desks — cigarette butts, chips and dips, French fries, and the remainder of a strawberry malt. The whole experience was exhilarating — to Butch, that is.

By the time 8:00 A.M. rolled around, Butch was wired. He was laughing uncontrollably. He kept up the hyena charade until every desk was cleaned. Then something bizarre happened. He handed each person a $100 bill. This behavior was typical, and as one employee put it, "You can't ever tell if you're gonna get kissed or kicked."

I added this story for one reason. Is your present boss worse than this? On the days you want to quit your job, turn to this chapter and compare your boss with Butch. If your boss is better than Butch, get back to work.

There is nothing, absolutely nothing, you can do to permanently change your boss's behavior. From the bad-breath boss to the boss who makes illegal requests, we've discussed them all, and you know what? If we surveyed the courageous people who *still* work for these detestable bosses, I'll bet those bosses haven't changed one bit.

The way to succeed with most bosses is to do what they ask you to do and don't talk about them behind their backs. If your boss makes you see red, instead of unloading on a co-worker, make plans to have dinner with a supportive friend, someone who will listen more than talk. Unpack that bag of resentment. Sometimes it is a big relief to spend time with someone who is willing to listen and not make immediate judgments.

If you have had several bad experiences with several bosses, it may be time for you to get some counseling. Most cities have counselors at not-for-profit job centers who can help you a great deal. One thing to remember is that you have control over your behavior and you also have some control over how you are treated.

That said, there's only one thing left to say. For things to change, you've gotta change.

Points to Remember

☐ Remember that your boss is your boss.

☐ If you don't get rid of negative images and feelings you have about your boss, you may be committing career suicide.

☐ Your boss's mood is not your business.

☐ Correcting your boss may be more embarrassing for you than it is for your boss.

☐ People do things for their own reasons, not yours.

☐ Judge people by their actions, not their words.

☐ No one can make you feel bad about yourself without your permission.

☐ Bad-mouthing the boss to others will get you nowhere.

☐ Do what your boss asks you to do unless it is illegal, immoral, or crosses your personal boundaries.

☐ For things to change, you've gotta change.

Best Bosses Finish First

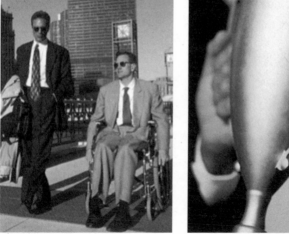

9

If you are a manager, supervisor, or owner of a small company, this chapter is for you. This chapter may dramatically change your work life. At the very least, it will help you cope with the work life you have.

If you are not a manager and would like some insight into what your boss deals with every day, you, too, will enjoy this chapter. Even if you don't care what your boss deals with on a daily basis but think that you are moving toward management yourself, then this will be of value to you.

Qualities of a Good Boss

To be a good boss, you need certain qualities. There are many opinions of what makes a good leader. I believe that leaders are made, not born. Good leaders have these qualities:

- Heart
- The ability to follow as well as lead
- Vision
- Consistency
- The desire to teach, to coach, and to watch people grow
- A willingness to set boundaries
- A willingness to hire people who are not like themselves

Heart

Having heart? Well, I learned that the hard way, and it took years. As a manager at age 23, I had the reputation of getting results at any cost. I was one of those people who was promoted because of a solid and dependable history of producing. I pushed myself hard, and I believed that the ends justified the means. I had my favorite pet phrases such as, "If you work, you stay, if you don't, you leave," "My way or the highway," and "Don't tell me about the labor pains, show me the baby."

> We have two ears and one mouth so that, as managers, we can listen twice as much as we talk.

A defining moment in my personal growth was when one of my salespeople had a daughter who was about to have surgery. Dawn was a single mother with a 10-year-old child. She was dependent on her success with our company. As a result, she was afraid of me and what I might do because of her being off work for the surgery. And rightly so; I wasn't known for leniency when it came to absenteeism. She was so afraid of being fired that she volunteered to make sales calls from the phone in her daughter's hospital room. I was thrilled and thought to myself, "What a trooper!"

When my boss got wind of Dawn setting up shop in the hospital, she was horrified. She tried to explain to me why my instilling this type of fear was not in the best interest of Dawn's daughter, Dawn, or me. I didn't really "hear" what she had to say for many years. She was talking about a concept that was not yet named — emotional intelligence.

In his book *EQ: Emotional Intelligence in Leadership and Organizations,* Dr. Robert Cooper says that the emotional quotient, EQ, underpins the most successful businesses and the most successful lives in this and in many other countries. He explains that the heart is just as important as the head in business. He believes that if we are not able to look for and honor the greatness in those around us, we can end up with empty lives.

Follow as well as Lead

Being a follower is how we all start out in our first job. Being a good follower means being teachable. Being teachable requires humility. Humility is that rare quality that allows us to know we don't know everything. Humility is the trait that allows us to fully listen to another human being.

Being a good follower is sometimes called being a good team player. To be a good team player, you sometimes have to sacrifice what you want for the good of the team. The next time you are working in a group, analyze your behavior. Are you talking twice as much as you are listening? Are you recognizing the others on your team as they make contributions? And most important, are you putting the needs of the group ahead of your own personal needs?

Vision

In a leadership context, having vision means dreaming about a better tomorrow. It's good for you to know how to deal effectively with the problems in front of you today. But as a leader, it's most important to have a vision for the future and a commitment to breathing life into your dream. It is most important that everyone who reports to you knows your vision. Your staff can help you with your plan, but you must communicate your vision in a way that everyone understands.

> **You can't motivate people. What you can do is create a healthy, open, and trusting environment in which people will motivate themselves.**

Consistency

Consistency was a hard one for me. As a new supervisor, I was always asking people to do a task and then forgetting what that task was. Because I forgot what I asked them to do, I would forget to follow up to see if they had done the task. Pretty soon, no one took me seriously, so I was angry about half of the time.

One day, I was driving in my car and listening to a management tape. The voice on the tape said: "If you don't follow up with your employees, you are ripping them off." That was a curious statement, I thought. What he meant was that if I didn't follow up and acknowledge good or bad completion of a task, I was taking away their ability to receive recognition. That day I made a decision to be consistent.

Up to that point in my career, I thought people should do what I wanted them to do because I was the boss. Period. With my new skill of consistency, I made a quantum leap as a supervisor. Around that time I also learned that "what gets measured gets done," so I designed a weekly reporting system. The system made my job easier and I was not constantly miffed. I also had a way to praise the best achievements of the week.

Teach, Coach, Watch People Grow

So far, we have talked about having heart, learning to follow, vision and consistency. This all comes together as you are able to sit back and watch your people grow within the boundaries you set. Management isn't always directives. A very large part of management is sitting back and watching your employees grow. In order to do this it is vital that you are an enthusiastic coach and a great trainer. Training takes time away from your job, and it is an investment that pays big dividends. If you don't get your kicks teaching, coaching, and watching people grow, you are not cut out for management.

> **If you don't get your kicks teaching, coaching, and watching people grow, you are not cut out for management.**

Set Boundaries

I'm embarrassed to say that in relationship to my long career, my ability to set boundaries for myself has come relatively late. To me, setting boundaries has been the hardest skill to learn. It is also well worth the time you will spend on it.

> **If you are supervising people and think you have no management problems, you are simply not paying attention.**

Part of setting boundaries means owning up to your feelings and being willing to talk about those feelings with those around you. For instance, if someone I work with hurts my feelings and I am playing the scene over and over in my head, it is up to me to talk with that person about it. Likewise, if an employee of mine is late to meetings time and again, it is up to me to have a talk with them.

You may have heard the saying "there are no victims in management, only volunteers." I believe this is true. If your staff is being sarcastic, obnoxious, or delegating up, it's up to you to ask them to correct their behavior. It is not up to them to figure it out on their own.

Hire People Not Like Yourself

When you read the last point in my good leader list, did you get a knot in your stomach? I said you must be willing to hire people who are not like you.

Let me explain. There is no way you can possibly know everything. It is your job to fill in your weaknesses with other people's strengths. For instance, if you are the "ready, fire, aim" type of leader rather than the "ready, aim, fire" type of leader, you need people around you who are good at planning and analyzing. On the other side of the coin, if you are a reserved, analytical leader, you will need a couple of people in your team who are spontaneous and exuberant. You may clash a little with them, but their strengths balance your weaknesses and make your company stronger as a whole.

Obnoxious Employees

As of today, I have never in my life talked to a boss who has no management problems. There are hostile, mean jerks, for example, opportunists who take advantage of your good nature, and employees who seem to have had no training in office etiquette. Then, of course, there are those who, to all appearances, are just lazy. I'll bet you have met some of these characters. You may even have a couple in your own office.

There are management problems and then there are management problems. Easily the most aggravating are the ones that exist solely because your employee is just plain obnoxious. I once had a manager in my company who couldn't stand people. Why did I promote her? As you read in Chapter Eight, I made the classic mistake of promoting my best producer and getting a mediocre manager. I eventually fired her, but before that I allowed her to make my work life miserable. You don't always have to fire obnoxious employees. You can't change them, but you may be able to alter the way they act in your office.

Hostile, Explosive Employee

Dear Jean,

I have an employee who is making me nuts. He is hostile, arrogant, and explosive. I "inherited" this employee, and I seem to resent his outbursts more every day. His work is superior — always has been. Very few people like him. They feel that he upsets the esprit de corps. So do I.

I have decided that I am not going to live with his behavior any longer. Either he becomes more pleasant in the office, or he's out of here. Here's my dilemma: I don't want to have this confrontation in my office. I have tried to talk with him and he storms out of the room when he hears something he doesn't like. I want him to stay for the entire discussion. Where should I have this meeting?

Reply:

To answer your question, many of the nicer hotels are now offering tea in the late afternoon. I can't think of a better setting or time. And who in his right mind would raise his voice or make an ugly scene in the dignified atmosphere of an afternoon tea?

If he is not a manager, maybe you can put this guy in a small room at the end of the hall. Perhaps you won't need to have that meeting. Out of sight, out of mind. Voilá! No more being made nuts.

Here's a response I received:

Dear Jean,

Boy, Jean. If I had an employee who had a tendency to blow up, the last place I would take him is "afternoon tea." This isn't England. How about just a normal old lunch?

> **Some employees brighten up a room by walking out of it.**

My reply:

A "normal old lunch" might not work as well. This exploder might just be too comfortable in this kind of atmosphere, comfortable enough to fall back on his usual method of dealing with disagreements. The idea of tea is to take him out of his comfort zone and put him on his best behavior. What about the public library?

"Limited" Vocabulary

Dear Jean,

I am the sales manager for a small company. As you can well imagine, the activity level runs really high. It's noisy, wild, and fun.

My problem is that the language in my office would make a sailor blush. I would need a calculator to count all the four-letter words I hear every day. I don't want to sound self-righteous. This has been a problem for me as well. The thing is, the sales department is right next to the reception area. I shudder to think what might happen if our best customer heard how limited our vocabulary is.

This issue was a topic at our last sales meeting. We all agreed we would cut this out. So far, I am the only person who has kept our agreement. This has to stop. What do I do?

Reply:

You're right. This is a time bomb. It's time to get creative. If everyone has agreed to stop and you have already stopped, the battle is halfway won. Breaking a bad habit requires an awareness of the habit.

What about a "cussing kitty"? Set up a system in which everyone who violates the agreement has to pay a rather hefty fine. Get everyone together to agree on the amount. Send the proceeds to a company-favored charity or have pizza delivered for an informal lunch.

Bad Grammar

Dear Jean,

I have an employee who is extremely capable and who does a wonderful job, but he cannot put a sentence together. No one else in the company complains, but this really bugs me. What do I do?

Reply:

First, you need to determine how important this is to you. If bad grammar will eventually cost this person his job, he needs to know right away. He also needs to know specifically what you want him to do to correct the problem. A private tutor or a class in grammar at a local college may be the answer.

There are three points for you to consider:

1. If you decide his grammar is not a deal breaker, focus on his good points and leave this one alone.

2. *You say he does a wonderful job? My dad used to warn me, "If it ain't broke, don't fix it."*

3. *If he is your biggest producer, you may want to convert all your other employees to: "It don't," "You was," and "We ain't."*

When wanting an employee to make a substantial change in behavior, consider this: How important is it? If a person who has bad grammar never sees a customer, never has occasion to write a memo, and never has complaints from anyone in the department, let it go. Use your energy on something else.

Consider Carefully before Firing an Employee

When you're just plain unhappy with an employee, firing seems easy enough, but before you do, acquaint yourself with the law. Federal laws apply to everyone, but state laws vary. To be safe, document every conversation you have with any employee regarding their job performance or questionable behavior.

Get That Religious Frenzy under Control!

Dear Jean,

I have an employee who is a religious zealot. She preaches on breaks and has Bible study in her office during the lunch hour. Neither I nor anyone else in the department can have a 10-minute conversation with her without her making reference to something that relates to her or her "church family."

This behavior is upsetting my whole team. I have talked to her about this, and for a while she straightened up. Now she's at it again. She's a good worker, but this is making us all nuts.

My boss told me to fire her if I couldn't get her religious frenzy under control. What do you think?

Reply:

It is not only politically incorrect, it is illegal to fire someone because of her religious beliefs. Because she is a good worker, I would suggest that the two of you find a way to work this out. Try talking with her once more. That will give you at least temporary relief, perhaps, and time to look for answers.

If you fire her, you may find yourself fighting a religious-discrimination charge. Just to be safe, call an attorney who is well acquainted with employment law. This may be one of the most cost-effective decisions you make this year.

Sexy Past with New Assistant

Dear Jean,

I was just introduced to my new assistant, handpicked by my old assistant, who is moving. To my shock and dismay, the girl happens to be a one-night stand of mine. To make matters worse, it wasn't a good experience. I am, of course, extremely uncomfortable with this situation. Do you have any advice on how to get rid of this girl?

Reply:

If you're wanting a legal answer, I can't help, but you would do well to quit calling her a "girl." I also wonder if you would plan to keep her if the one-night stand had been a good experience.

If you are wanting my opinion, here goes: If her work is as lousy as your one-night stand, you will have a legitimate reason to fire her. Of course, if she was as disenchanted with you as you were with her, she'll probably quit anyway. Otherwise, make your expectations clear and get back to business.

By the way, next time, have your assistant refer the top two or three candidates to you so you can choose your own employee.

Management Issues

Maybe you have read books on management. I have. Most of them, although stuffed full of theory, are lacking when it comes to dealing with the issues that are happening in front of you. There is the employee who is borrowing (without permission) the company's portable computer to make a presentation to an antique-car club over the weekend. What about the receptionist who has found a way to access your cable TV on her computer and is watching while the front-desk phones are ringing off the hook?

Borrowing Is Stealing

Dear Jean,

One of my employees took home a VCR from our office without asking. I don't think this is right. Am I over-reacting?

Reply:

No, you're not. This is serious. Would someone take something from your home and act blasé? Meet with the employee today and ask that he or she not do this again. If the VCR isn't returned promptly, call the police. That's not borrowing, that's stealing!

This employee has a sense of entitlement that he is clearly not entitled to. Failure to nip this unofficial "borrowing" in the bud can lead to more questionable infringements down the road. This is especially dangerous if you have a large office or department. Without sounding awfully jaded, let me leave you with a cliché: "Monkey see, monkey do!"

Tardy Again

Dear Jean,

I have an employee who is late several times a week. I've never said any-

thing to him, and his co-workers are starting to resent his tardiness. How do I approach this problem?

Reply:

Part of your role as a supervisor is to act as a problem solver. Get with him and calmly explain why this behavior is not acceptable and that it has a negative impact on the group. Find out if there is a reason for his continual late arrival. It is possible that his day-care center won't accept his child until a certain time, and this throws him off schedule. Discuss ideas for on-time arrival. Let him tell you what he plans to do to correct this behavior. Set a date to review progress. On the other hand, if he's your most valuable employee, you may want to have the meeting and the review with the rest of your staff to explain why you're cutting some slack for Mr. Hot Shot.

Here is a response to that question and answer:

Dear Jean,

I just thought I'd write a note on the side of arriving after 8:00 A.M. to work. The workday is changing shape. More people are starting work after 8:00 A.M. and staying at work until 6:00 P.M., 7:00 P.M., or even later. Because the world is moving toward a 24-hour day, being flexible with hours can have huge benefits in the workplace.

Many people do not do their best work that early in the morning. They work better in the afternoons or at night. Managers who want the most work done need to start looking less at the time clock and more at their employees' work styles. Lighten up.

My reply:

Despite the movement toward a 24-hour business day, the accepted office business hours are still 8:00 A.M. to 5:00 P.M. This is not likely to change very quickly. It is also important to take into account the work of the company as a whole. Getting to work on time becomes extremely important in an office where your customer can be contacted only between 8:00 A.M. and 5:00 P.M., or where people are actually working as a team. If one person is late, it holds up the work of the entire team. It is not asking too much to expect an employee to be at work on time.

Loose Behavior Makes Company Look Bad

Dear Jean,

I just discovered that several of my employees have been meeting at bars after work on a social basis. This in itself is not a real problem, but apparently they have also been going home together in pairs and coming in to work together late the next day. This is costing me quite a bit in "gossip time" throughout the office. This loose behavior also reflects poorly on the company. What steps can I take to minimize this problem?

Reply:

If you can figure out how to control your employees' after-hours activities, write a book. Soon you'll be in the presidential suite at an exotic resort sipping a cool drink on the beach.

If you are like most of us, you have no control over what people do. As for the loss of productivity, if they have so much time on their hands and can gossip all day, they don't have enough work to do. All you can do is measure their work. You are in no position to measure their morality.

Trouble with My Intern

Dear Jean,

I have about had it with my intern. She misses deadlines, is late to work, and interrupts her co-workers with personal conversation. We have discussed this several times. She just doesn't get the picture. What do I do now? She is smart and is married to my cousin.

Reply:

It doesn't matter much whom she is married to. You have a serious problem that will undoubtedly get worse if you don't take action.

State the problem as you see it. Ask for the reason she has not corrected her behavior. Don't fall for a smooth story; stay objective. If her reason for noncompliance is anything less than a family or personal tragedy, tell her you are putting her on a 90-day probation. State the terms of the probation and follow up every week until the behavior changes, or until you give her notice to look for a new position. If the talking does not stop, you will have to assume that she will be happier elsewhere. Even if she is not happier if she goes elsewhere, you will be. So will your staff members, who have been watching you put up with this noncompliant person.

Be Clear about Expectations

In the chapter on career advice, I stressed the fact that you never get a second chance at a first impression. That goes for managers and companies, too.

When a new employee comes on board, consider meeting with him to discuss your expectations. The time it takes you to do this will be made up a hundredfold.

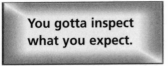

You gotta inspect what you expect.

Be very clear about what you expect of him in all areas. While you are at it, write down what he can expect of you. Here's what I discuss with every new employee:

WHAT I EXPECT FROM YOU

I expect you to :
- be consistent in your work, especially in regard to our "system."
- tell the truth in matters affecting your position.
- produce prompt, deadline-sensitive work.
- be at work when the whole team starts at 8:00 A.M.
- honor your lunch hour and not make arrangements to trade without approval.

- defend my philosophy within the office and in the community.
- be dedicated and committed to your position as outlined by your supervisor.
- honor confidentiality with respect to intraoffice matters, i.e., gross margins, trade secrets, employee salaries, etc. (among employees as well as outsiders).
- not get into long conversations about your personal life.
- keep personal telephone calls to a minimum.
- join our team approach. I want you to solve problems for me, not make them.
- tell me IMMEDIATELY if there has been an uncomfortable situation with any of our clients or customers.
- abide by the federal and state laws in regard to the individuals with whom we work. This applies to applicants, temporaries, and clients. This includes derogatory comments in relation to race, religion, or sexual orientation.

WHAT YOU CAN EXPECT FROM ME

You can expect:

- that you will be a great deal more marketable as a result of your tenure here.
- that your payroll check will be on time and not bounce.
- that these doors will be open every day and you will have a place to come to work.
- that your written employment agreements will be honored unless changes are agreed on by both parties.
- that you will have an opportunity to be promoted, providing you have the qualifications for the position.
- to be praised for work above and beyond the call of duty.
- educational opportunities and social opportunities.
- that I will be pleasant and positive 80 percent of the time.
- that I will explore all possibilities when making a decision that affects your position or income.

- that if you are having a problem with someone in the office, I will pull you both in for a discussion.
- confidentiality when you specifically ask for it.
- a response to any personal or business crisis.
- me not to be angry or put off if you have a family crisis and cannot be at work.
- to have a day off with pay if you're exhausted.
- to receive a week's vacation every six months or to be paid for the time if you don't take the vacation.
- me not to ask you to change your vacation at the last minute.
- a willing ear for well-thought-out (written) suggestions.
- that all office equipment will be properly maintained and updated as needed to conduct business in the most efficient manner possible.
- no generational chauvinism.

Boundaries

Watching a 3-year-old test her mother's limits is a lesson in management. Your team will find a new way to test your limits every week. What happens when a 3-year-old bites and hits her mother? The mother becomes very focused and sets a boundary with a swift and sure consequence. The very next time the child bites or hits, the competent mother rises to the occasion and enforces the consequence.

When a child is misbehaving, most parents have no problem setting boundaries. Enforcing them is another kettle of fish. We seem to expect things to be different at the office. We expect that people in an office know how to act. When a child repeatedly crosses boundaries and does not have to suffer consequences, the child becomes impossible to handle. Employees do, too. In an office, this type of drama is complicated by the fact that morale drops when one or two people don't have to play by the rules. Esprit de corps is wrecked and tension mounts.

There are boundaries and there are deal breakers. Deal breakers are things people do that result in their getting fired. In our office, a deal breaker is the mistreatment of a customer or client. Another deal breaker is violent behavior toward a fellow employee.

> **Deal breakers are things people do that result in their getting fired.**

In some offices, being tardy is a deal breaker. For example, in the airline industry, where the company philosophy is to be on time every time, tardiness is an issue. As you read the following questions and answers, give some thought to the differences between irritating behavior and behavior that constitutes a deal breaker.

Heavy Metal Music at the Front Desk

Dear Jean,

When we hired our receptionist, she appeared to be wholesome. Within the last couple of months, she has dyed her hair a Kool-Aid orange and purchased a multicolor snake tattoo which was artfully installed on her ankle. The tongue piercing will probably be next. She has gone from the girl next door to the nightmare on Lincoln Avenue.

I can deal with the colorful getup because we have virtually no walk-in traffic. The thing that gets my goat is the radio at the front desk. The metal music that is blasting out of the speakers is more than heavy!! Several customers have complained when they called in to speak with me.

The owner of the company is ultra laid back and a pretty good guy, so I wouldn't have a problem telling him my concern, but this young lady is his niece. What do I do?

Reply:

Theoretically, whom the owner hires and what she does is not your business, but when it affects your customers' perceptions and, therefore, your earnings, it becomes a different matter.

I am curious as to why the owner of the company is wearing those blinders. There are only a few reasons why this has been allowed to go on. 1. He hasn't noticed. 2. He doesn't care. 3. He is hesitant to confront her. 4. He has been smoking barbershop shavings. 5. The young lady's mother is his favorite sister.

No matter what the reason, if this is causing you concern, it's important that you have a talk with him. Be careful to stay coolheaded. Stick with what you have seen and heard. Avoid judgmental comments.

Kids in the Office

Dear Jean,

The guy in the office down the hall invites his wife and kids to the office several times a week. Now my assistant has started to allow her kid to pop in after school once in a while. I don't think spouses and children belong in a working office. How should I handle this problem, or is it a problem? Am I simply behind the times?

Reply:

Probably not. I wonder how we would feel if our dentist allowed his/her children to hang out in the office during a sensitive procedure, or any procedure? I know this example is a bit dramatic, but it makes the point, doesn't it?

Because you have no control over the guy down the hall, your best bet is to ignore his wife and children. Where your assistant is concerned, ask her to stop allowing her child to hang around in the office. Do it in a straightforward manner.

Please avoid the urge to be self-righteous. Explain that this behavior is not in her best interest. It is up to you to set the tone for your own office. Explain that in most offices, you can go up the ladder a lot faster with the more traditional approach when it comes to visitors.

TV on the Job

Dear Jean,

I work in a small law firm. I have had only three administrative assistants in my whole career, so I don't stay "in the know" when it comes to supervisory issues.

My present assistant has slipped a small TV into her office. She's a pretty good worker, but I suspect from the sounds I hear in the hall outside her office that she is keeping current with her favorite soaps. I don't want to be seen as the bad guy, but Jean, is this sort of thing accepted in other offices?

Reply:

This might be accepted in some offices, but it doesn't have to be accepted in yours. If she is watching TV an hour a day, that amounts to six-and-a-half workweeks a year.

Some people call that type of behavior "stealing from the company." If this issue is important to you, ask her to stop. Explain that "watching while you work" may be fine in other parts of the company, but it is not acceptable to you.

It's a good idea to get this done right away, before the senior partner gets wind of entertainment alley down your way.

Soaps at Lunch

Dear Jean,

I am the senior partner in a law firm. I am fairly laid back, and most people consider me reasonably tolerant. Last week at about 12:30 P.M., I walked by our conference room, and several of our clerical employees were watching soap operas on the television we use to show training videos. I am usually with clients at this time of day, so I don't know how long this has been going on. I would like it to stop. Am I being an old fuddy-duddy?

Reply:

Although there is no right answer to this, there may be some groundwork for you to lay before running into this head-on. Maybe one of your partners approved this lunch-hour activity. If not, it may be wise to examine why you feel this way. Do clients visit your office at lunch? Are you wanting to control what your employees do on their lunch hour? Are employees returning to their desks on time? Do you need to use the conference room? Is there a policy against this? If you want this stopped, you can take care of it right away. After all, it is your TV.

Here is a response I received:

Dear Jean,

My lunch hour is my lunch hour, and if I want to watch my soaps, I have that right. I resent people like you infringing on my personal time. That's what's wrong with this country, people like you who think they know what's best for someone else's personal time.

My reply:

Your employer really does have a right to tell you what is acceptable on his property and in using his property, regardless of whether you are using work time or your personal time. Maybe you will want to bring your own TV — and watch it in your car.

Could It Be Your Fault?

There are many situations in which you have an employee who is making you nuts, and it's not the employee's fault. Sometimes you have to fire people, but before you do, be sure to examine if you're unhappy about something that is really your fault. Because you are the boss, it's up to you to teach your staff how to respond to your expectations.

Delegating Up

Dear Jean,

I have an employee who is always delegating up and asking me to do things for him. What should I tell him?

Reply:

The best thing to do is examine what there is in your present or past behavior that is causing this to happen. Have you had sufficient management training? Are you trying to be a buddy? Have you been extremely clear on your expectations? Have you hired the wrong person? My guess is that this person is not clear on what the boundaries are. Make sure he knows specifically what you want him to do or not do.

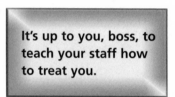

It's up to you, boss, to teach your staff how to treat you.

Tell him you wouldn't dream of interfering in his work, and ship the project right back to him. Tell him you'll look at the finished product with great interest. The ball is now in his court.

I Work for My Assistant

Dear Jean,

My assistant and I are having a war. She thinks I work for her. Every week, I have a memo on my desk telling me how she wants to organize my week. I have been at my work a number of years, and I resent this intrusion. I don't want to appear hostile, but this has to stop. What should I tell her the next time she gives me a new suggestion on how to run my life?

Reply:

Avoid waiting until the next time she ruffles your feathers. Talk with her now. The longer you wait, the more resentment you will be building. It will be useful for you to practice the technique of "I feel _____ when you _____. Please _____."

Here's how it might sound: "I feel resentful when you attempt to organize everything I do. Please don't write me memos. If you would like to have a conversation about how you could be helpful to me, I will be happy to discuss anything you have on your mind."

Important! You must remain calm. The calmer you are, the more impact this will have. Practice this until you can say the words without any anger in your voice. Diplomacy is the key. Remember that you are the employer and you will be setting the tone for this confrontation, so be sure to keep your cool. Being unduly hard on her won't help her or you. Her effort to organize you may be coming from a sincere desire to help you or from her experiences on a previous job.

The Untrained Temp

Dear Jean,

My boss asked me to order a temp to fill in at our front desk. When I called the service, I asked for someone who can answer four incoming lines. The temporary service sent out a perfectly charming person. She does a good job with the phones, but that is all she can do, and I mean that is all she can do.

I gave her a typing project, and she didn't even know how to put the paper into the typewriter. I'd like to assume that the fax is not too much of a stretch for anyone, but it is for her. Am I way off base to expect our receptionist to do more than answer the phone?

Reply:

You're not off base to expect your receptionist to have varied office skills, but you did need to be specific when you ordered the temp — really specific.

Next time you call the service, make a list of everything you know for a fact she or he will be doing. If the temporary will be using a copier, write that down. If you think it's important to have experience on a fax, write that down. If the temp has to use a typewriter, make sure you ask for someone with typewriter experience.

Because many people coming out of school learned the keyboard on a computer and most offices now don't even have a typewriter, it's critical that you be specific! I'm sure all this sounds pretty basic, but consider: Well over 50 percent of temporary-worker failures result from a lack of clear expectations when the order is called in. As you know, hiring a temp who cannot do what you need done is like throwing $20 bills out the window. An extra 10 minutes of conversation with your supplier of temporaries will save you a lot of $20s. The results of your chat may also make you look good, because the receptionist's good work will reflect on you.

Training

More new hires have failed because of lack of proper training than any other thing. It's always seemed odd to me that we are willing to invest beaucoup bucks in a new hire and then we assist with an attitude of "sink or swim, nobody trained me, I made it and look at me."

> **Every minute you spend in training will save you 15 minutes in the first month.**

A training program should be well thought out. It starts on the first day with a complete orientation. Here is the guide I use with our customers who have no formal training or orientation program for front-desk receptionists. Even though this orientation is for receptionists, you can use this as a model for almost any position. *(See illustration page 254-255)*

RECEPTIONIST QUICK REFERENCE GUIDE

GENERAL INFORMATION

I report to: _____

Office hours: _____

Lunch break: _____

Physical address: _____

_____

Post office box: _____

Phone number: _____

Fax number: _____

Company product or service:_____

_____

PHONE INSTRUCTIONS

Exact words used to answer the phone: _____

_____

How to transfer a call: _____

How to dial intraoffice: _____

Intraoffice directory and organizational chart: _____

_____

MISCELLANEOUS INFORMATION

Guidelines for handling appointments, guests, or walk-ins:

_____

_____

Method for handling the mail:_____

Guidelines for personal phone calls: _____

If you need to leave the front desk:_____

_____

Other important information:

_____

_____

_____

_____

_____

_____

_____

_____

_____

_____

Much of what a new employee learns is "on the job." Because there will be many things that your new hire can learn only by doing, make it a point to have an open-door policy. If you are not the person who is doing the training, make sure the person who is makes time available each day for the new hire. Training is an investment. Remember how you learned to read or do math? It was by spaced repetition. Use that technique for training.

Smart New Employee Doesn't Get It

Dear Jean,

After three weeks of training a new employee, I am ready to tear my hair out. We are just not on the same wavelength. I tell him something to do, and the next day he does something else. The man is smart and has good references. I have never had this problem before. I am stumped!

Reply:

Based on the information you gave me, I am stumped, too. Let's consider four general possible reasons why he is not doing what you ask him to do.

1. He is impaired by drugs.

2. He has personal problems.

3. He is defiant.

4. You are not saying it in a way he can hear it.

Some people listen in a linear way and some in a more global, big-picture way. If you are linear and he is global, he is asleep by the time you finish telling him the steps. He needs to hear the bottom line first and then work backward. If you are global and he is linear, you won't be sequential enough for him to understand you. You will have to make sure your instructions are in sequence, no-big-picture, no-bottom-line stuff. If that doesn't work, you will have to replace him.

Here's a response I got:

Dear Jean,

What is with this "linear" and "global" mumbo jumbo? Either he gets it or he doesn't. It is as simple as that. It is up to the employee to learn from the manager or lose his job if he can't learn the stuff. I wouldn't have time to analyze everything I say to a new employee just to figure out whether it will mesh with the way he "listens." I don't think anyone has that kind of time. Really, Jean, give some advice we can use.

My reply:

Although it is difficult to listen to people and pay attention to the way they think, the rewards are huge. Not everyone thinks in the same way. If you can learn to adapt to others' ways of thinking, you will make yourself understood by them much easier. This will save you countless hours of training time.

Correcting an Employee

Dear Jean,

I am training someone in our office. How do I get it across to this girl that she is doing much of her work wrong? I have talked to my boss, and he is no help. He keeps telling me I am doing fine. Obviously, I am not doing fine or this new trainee would be up to speed. I learned the job in three days. She's already on day five.

Reply:

No two people learn at the same speed. Because you so were quick to learn your job means that you may be a little more impatient with people who have a learning style that is different from yours.

Correcting an employee is difficult, but with a little practice it will become almost easy. The most important part of correcting behavior is to state the behavior change in the positive. Rather than saying, "You are preparing this document wrong," say, "Here is how to prepare this document correctly."

As I mentioned, this technique takes time and practice, but believe me, the benefits far outweigh the time it takes to learn this skill. You'll be glad you did. I promise.

How to Rally Your Temps

Dear Jean,

I have been working for a company that uses temporaries extensively. Last week, I was given the use of three temps to help complete a large project. Human Resources makes the selections. Sometimes they send me morons. This project has to be done in three months. It's a significant undertaking. How do I get these temps to rally around the needs of our department and the needs of our customers?

Reply:

Most likely, HR will send you three temporaries who are technically qualified to help you complete your project. If they are not qualified, it may be because you were not specific enough when you sent in the request for the temporaries. I am not ruling out incompetence on the part of your HR staff, but most of the time when an error is made in relationship to temps, it is because of poor communication.

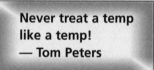

Never treat a temp like a temp!
— Tom Peters

After you have determined the capabilities of your temporaries, make a plan and get right to work. The way you orient your new staff members will determine their work output and how well they rally around your needs.

Be sure everyone on the project knows what results are expected and how you plan to measure those results. If you put your expectations in writing, there is very little chance of being misunderstood. The more specific the better. Avoid letting yourself be tempted to just hand them the piece of paper. Sit down with each team member to explain what you wrote and how each point applies to them.

In Tom Peters' book The Pursuit of Wow!, *he writes, "Treat temporaries like you would a permanent employee. Welcome them into your company, show them respect and trust, give them real responsibilities, let them develop their own strategies and hold them to the same high standards. This is the secret of success at places like Disney where turnover is enormous. Training and reward systems (and bosses) treat the 90-day employee just the same as if he or she were going to be there 20 years."*

Peters sums it up by saying, "Never treat a temp like a temp!"

Employee Motivation

All people are motivated. Yes, you heard me right. All people are motivated. They may not be motivated to do what you want them to do, but they are in fact motivated.

When I was new in management, I thought people would do what I wanted them to do because I said so. Wrong. I liked the word boss and I was thrilled to be one. The only thing I knew about bossing was to boss everyone around. There's a word for my old management style — *dictatorial.*

My bull-in-a-china-closet style eventually forced me to read many books on the subject of management. I learned that to manage others, I must first learn to manage myself well. I learned that to be effective, I must set an example, and that people want to be led, not managed.

Many books have been written on management and leadership. The book that comes to mind as having the most valuable information on management-building skills is *The Greatest Management Principle*, by Michael Lebouf. Lebouf taught me what I consider the most important thing a manager must know to be successful. To be a successful manager, you must know that if you want someone to perform any type of

> **Your entire staff is listening to the same radio station, WIIFM — What's in It for Me?**

function, you must measure the results.

You must be saying, "That sounds way too much like baby-sitting. No way, not me, I won't do that. I hired competent people and I expect them to perform without my involvement." If this is exactly how you feel, you will learn this lesson exactly as I did, through massive turnover.

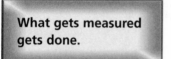

What gets measured gets done.

From reading *The Greatest Management Principle*, I also figured out that it is a rip-off to ask an employee to perform a special assignment and then not recognize the contribution. I used to think that a paycheck was the thanks my staff wanted and needed. Wrong again. People do want fair compensation, but beyond that, it's recognition they want. Some people want standing ovations and some want a verbal pat on the back. Some people want very little attention drawn to them, so a sealed note would work just as well. What we all have in common is that we want to feel important. If you don't make your employees feel important, they will go to work for someone who will. Remember, people do things for their own reasons, not yours.

Getting Back on Track

Dear Jean,

Our company has been through tremendous change. We were acquired by a large public firm. There have been reductions in the number employed here. All we have left is low morale and low productivity. These changes, I might add, were all in the name of "continuous improvement."

My staff's low productivity is the reason for my letter. Through a strange twist of fate, no one in my department was terminated, and we are starting the process of "re-engineering." How can I get my staff back on track?

Reply:

In his book, Do Lunch or Be Lunch, *Howard H. Stevenson, a professor* at Harvard Business School, writes that we as humans have a deep desire to predict and shape the future. He also says we have the desire to predict the behavior of those around us.

Getting back on track means that you will first have to help your staff deal with the anger and grief they are feeling as a result of the changes. They will be acting out of fear, so let them talk out their fears with you. Set aside a time to meet with everyone personally. Low morale is expected when employees see their friends and colleagues lose their jobs. They will be looking to you for support, just as you will be looking to your boss.

You have a right to expect that the work will be done in your department. Even though you have no control over how your staff will integrate these changes emotionally, you must hold them accountable for their productivity.

By now, your boss should have given you some specifics about what is expected of your work group. It's time for you to let your expectations be known as well. Let your staff help determine the steps you will take together to reach your goals. Construct a time line to measure your results.

It is up to you as the leader to provide some sense of predictability. Start with rituals. Even the smallest rituals will seem to bring back the predictability that all of you desire. A short weekly meeting at which you recognize contributions from your team members might be a good place to begin.

Whatever you decide to do to bring back some stability to your department has to be done religiously. If it is not done religiously, you may become part of the problem rather than part of the solution.

As for your career, head for the rapids. Read, study, and be open to new ideas. Even though this may be a nerve-racking ride, your chances of capsizing are far less if you paddle like crazy and go with the flow.

In closing, Stevenson also says, "Re-engineering means that the rules are changing. And 'continuous improvement' means that the rules will continue to change."

We Want Her to Stay

Dear Jean,

We have a receptionist/secretary in our office who is a wonderful worker, but she has decided she is going to quit. Everyone in the office is really upset about it because she is such a fabulous person. There is some tension she is having to deal with as the receptionist, so I am wondering if there is anything the rest of us can do to make her feel more comfortable and convince her to stay.

Reply:

You are one of the few people who recognizes how valuable a good receptionist is, and I am glad you are heading the campaign to encourage her to stay.

With the exception of personal problems, the main reason people leave jobs is because their needs are not getting met. She is obviously not getting her needs met, and asking her is the only way to find out what those needs are.

Get with her boss right away and tell him or her that you and the whole staff would like to see this wonderful person stay. Once the boss finds out what her needs are — the ones that are not getting met — you and she might have a chance of keeping this great receptionist. Have you considered tying her to her chair?

Staff Resistance

Dear Jean,

I'm in a real mess. Our company is going through a major system change and my staff is resisting like crazy. I know how they feel. I was mortified when I first learned of this major change. I'm used to the idea now, you might even say I've bought in, but how do I sell this to my staff?

Reply:

You will need to describe why the changes need to be made. Remember that your staff listens to that radio station WIIFM, meaning "What's in It for Me." Tell them how they can personally benefit from the change, then wait for a reaction. No matter what they have to say, listen carefully. You will then be able to fill in any gaps in communication. As you close, ask that they support the change whether they like it or not.

> **Picture all of your employees walking around with big signs around their necks that say, "Make Me Feel Important!"**

It's important that they have a chance to tell their whole story in your presence. Yes, this type of listening is laborious. The benefit to you for listening to them is that it will be much easier for them to let the drama subside after they are sure you have completely heard and understood their side of the issue.

Staff Motivation

Dear Jean,

Our company just went through a merger. Three companies were merged into one. Our surviving company, which was the largest before the merger, seems to be the one taking the hardest hit. We are having to make more changes than the other two companies. We are adapting to that, but morale throughout the complete new company has dropped to almost rock bottom.

We get a lot of indecision from the CEO and management of the organization. It seems there is a lot of deadwood up there. As I said, morale has dropped. As a department head myself, I'm having a hard time keeping my staff motivated. What can I do?

Reply:

Change is hard for everyone, and I'm really glad you're the type of manager who wants to be inspirational.

If you can add lightness to the workplace, you will be far ahead. Once, we went through an especially rough time when morale was low. We covered an empty Kleenex box with colored paper and called it the "brag box." Each week, everyone in the company entered the name of the co-worker who went above and beyond the call of duty. Each Friday, we read all the brags during our staff meeting. It was a real upper! Maybe it will work for your group.

Dysfunctional Employees

Dear Jean,

Recently, I read an article in a major magazine about supervising people from "dysfunctional families." What are dysfunctional families, and am I really supposed to treat these people differently?

Reply:

A dysfunctional family is a family that does not perform in a required or expected manner. Dysfunction is caused by many things: alcoholism, drugs, physical or emotional abuse, incest, gambling, suicide, obsessive spending, and poverty, to name a few.

There has been a lot of publicity on dysfunctional families in the last 10 years. If we are really honest with ourselves, nearly all of us have been touched in one way or another by one of these challenges in our own families. To the extent that all people are individuals, these staff members should be treated differently. However, if you are talking about cutting them slack, the answer is absolutely not.

It is really important that everyone knows what your expectations are of each of them as an employee. You as a manager need to treat each person fairly no matter what the circumstances.

Here is a response to that letter:

Go, Jean!!

It's about time we started paying less attention to all those users who try to get away with stuff at work by saying (with tears in their eyes) that they come from a "dysfunctional family" or they are "having personal problems right now" or any one of the hundreds of weak excuses we hear. I'm sick to death of hearing all of that. I've had my share of problems, too, but you don't hear me bitching about it. I work hard anyway. Maybe if I started bitching about my problems, I'd get more sympathy — and even a raise!

Managing Volunteers

Dear Jean,

My wife does volunteer work for a couple of organizations, and she has been given the privilege of being president of the board. I think this is more title than anything else, because when she tries to do anything, the problem she runs into all the time is lack of motivation among the other volunteers.

> **If you want to know how effective you are as a manager, try managing volunteers.**

She'll make a list of tasks for each of them to do and they will just look at her like, "Yeah, right. We're not doing this!" There's one salaried employee who is supposed to answer to and interact with my wife, but when my wife suggests things or tries to get something done, this employee just ignores her, blows her off, or acts as though she doesn't remember the request.

My idea is just to fire everybody, run everybody off, and get a whole new crew that will work. Do you have a more diplomatic suggestion?

Reply:

Yes. What you have to remember is that these volunteers are volunteers. They don't have to work; they aren't paid. So if you "fire" all the volunteers, my guess is that you will get the same type of people back, if you get anyone!

Your wife's staff person is another case; it's obvious there is a serious problem between your wife and her. The best scenario is that they just got off to a bad start. The worst scenario is that this person balks at any kind of authority. Is there any way your wife can talk to the previous president *about how to work best with this person?*

Your wife will benefit from some leadership training. The book How to Win Friends and Influence People, *a classic by Dale Carnegie, has a lot of great leadership ideas.* Leader Effectiveness Training *is a good one, too.*

Let's talk about you, as well! It's great that you care about your wife's dilemma. The best thing you can do for her is give her the names of these books. Try your best not to "fix" anything for her. Women's number-two complaint about men is that they don't listen. Most of the time women only want their husbands to listen. Listening doesn't require action of any kind.

By the way, your wife sounds capable. If she weren't, she wouldn't have been chosen to be president.

Accused of Not Listening

Dear Jean,

I have been accused of not listening. My employees, my husband, and my children all think I don't listen to them. Granted, I'm pretty intense most of the time, and it is true that once in a while I don't completely understand what they've said. I'm not even sure I want to do a great deal more listening. I have made it this far, to "senior management," so why do I have to change?

Reply:

You don't have to change, unless you want a smoother, less complicated life. Because you have the courage to write, I feel that you are ready to make some positive changes in your listening style (I didn't say changes in your personality).

Unless you make it a priority to hear and fully understand people, you won't be able to do it. Make sure that you are in the frame of mind to listen. If you are faking it, your nonverbal communication will give you away. If you respond so quickly that you step on their last word, you will not have processed the whole meaning of what they have said. To make sure they know you heard them, count to three before you respond. Listen for both the fact and the body language associated with the message, then paraphrase what they just told you to confirm that you understand what they are thinking, feeling, and saying.

Cooing and Coddling

Dear Jean,

My boss tells me that I have no people skills. She says that if I become better at motivating people, I will have a rewarding future with my company. If I don't, I'm history.

I am working about 50 hours a week and, quite frankly, I don't have the time to be coddling my staff. They are all adults, and I resent the fact that they seem to need special attention.

Five people report directly to me, and they are always going behind my back and ratting to my boss about my lack of what I call "warm fuzzies." I believe we are here to do business and not to make friends. This whole deal is making me miserable. What do you think I should do?

Reply:

Your boss has been very clear with you, so you have a decision to make. You will either have to get some skill training or spiff up your resume.

There is this problem, however. If you choose to find another management position, you may end up working for the same type of boss that you have now! And you will be right back to square one.

Would it hurt you to hand out a few "warm fuzzies"? If you do, the return could be great. If you don't, the results could be cataclysmic — for you. It sounds to me very much like, "Be nice or be gone!"

I can tell by your letter that you are an intensely task-oriented person, that accomplishing your objectives is your highest priority. If you will be willing to carve out five minutes every day in the effort to create a motivational environment, your relationship with your staff and with your boss *will change immediately.*

Here are some short phrases to use every time you catch one of your staff members doing something right.

Way to go — Now you've got it — Bravo — Bingo — You're a winner — That's incredible — You're remarkable — You're on target — Dynamite — Super job — Nice job — Good job — You're absolutely right — You're on your way — How smart of you — You're very thoughtful — Hooray for you — You are unique — You're OK — Amazing piece of work — You're a real trooper — I see you're burning that midnight oil — Thank you!

Use these phrases religiously for 30 days. If they don't work, I'll gladly refund your misery.

Triangulation

There is a term called *triangulation*. Triangulation (rhymes with strangulation) occurs when there are three people involved in a two-person conflict. Avoid this, and you will sleep better every night.

Feuding Subordinates

Dear Jean,

Two of the people who report to me are not getting along. Every day, I hear an update on their cold war. How do I stop this war?

Reply:

One of the most unproductive things in business is engaging in this type of activity. Whether you are in the cold war or are the sounding board for someone who is, this is costly. One thing you must do is get out of that triangle today.

Call a meeting with the two who are involved. Explain that they don't have to like each other, but they do have to act courteously and be helpful to each other as far as company projects are concerned. Make it perfectly clear that they may not come to you about a problem regarding the other person unless they have discussed the problem with the other person first.

If you continue to be a party to this feud, you become a part of the problem rather than part of the solution. Set a review date to check progress.

Warring Managers

Dear Jean,

Two of my key managers are having a private war. To retaliate, they purposefully leave one another out of the feedback loop. Most of their time is spent trying to find the missing part so they can complete deadlines. This is making me nuts. I would fire them both if they were not so valuable. Short of firing them, what can I do?

Reply:

Call a meeting. Everyone must acknowledge that a problem exists. Get the problem out on the table and propose an approach to solving it. Make sure your managers realize that you know the impact it is having on their performances.

Ask them to brainstorm solutions. As they explore different options, write the ideas down and help your employees work toward a solution that will resolve the conflict and increase performance. After 10 or 15 minutes, start guiding them toward closure and a consensus in regard to resolving the conflict and increasing performance.

Decide on a date to review the conflict and the managers' performance. Be sure to follow up on that particular day. If you don't, you will be sending a message that you don't really mean business.

Writing a Reference Letter

Once in a while you will be asked to write a reference letter. Every excellent reference letter I receive I put in a file folder. That way when I am asked to write a reference letter, I don't have to start from scratch. I can use these letters as a guide. Here's an example:

Dear Mr. Smith:

Nicole Harvet has worked for the Jean Kelley Companies for the last couple of years. She has worn many hats. Her primary responsibilities have been:

(fill in responsibilities here)

There are many things that are special about Nicole. With her quiet, sincere demeanor, she wears well with a number of different types of personalities. Her co-workers are especially fond of her. She "delivers" on time, every time. There is not a person in our company who does not respect her.

Nicole consistently exceeds expectations in every area. She is smart, quick, and pleasant. As a matter of fact, she is so bright that she makes her supervisors stretch to keep up with her, myself included. Additionally, she has (without request) improved and enhanced several of the systems related to her position.

If you are looking for a punctual, dependable fast-tracker with a solid record of achievement, Nicole Harvet is your person.

Sincerely,

Jean Kelley
President

Writing a Good Reference Letter

Dear Jean,

I have had the same secretary for 10 years. Because of a family problem, she is leaving the state. She has asked me for a letter of reference. Having never written a letter of reference, I'm stumped as to what to put in it. It's not my nature to go on and on with glowing compliments. As a matter of fact, I'm suspicious when I read letters like that. June has been a nearly perfect assistant. Can you give me some guidelines?

Reply:

Letters carried by the employee don't cut much ice with prospective employers anyway, so you have time on your side. Assure June that you will indeed write such a letter as soon as you're contacted by the company(ies) to which she applies.

Now write down, in list form, all the things that June does well. Are you sorry to see her go? Write that down. Would you hire her again? Write your answer down. Will her family problem interfere with her business life? Write your answer down. Now you have the raw material from which to build a good, well-thought-out reference letter. Keep a copy. You may be required to write more than one letter for June. You owe that to her. By the way, there is nothing wrong with a glowing reference if it's merited.

As you can see from reading this last chapter, being a good leader is more than telling people what to do. Management and leadership take serious work. The days you are not dealing with difficult employees, you are dealing with a challenging boss. Some days you feel like you're in a vise, the kind that squeezes. Your boss is demanding results of you, and your job is to get people to rise to your level of expectations. This is not a career choice for wimps.

Points to Remember

☐ You can't motivate people. You can, however, create an environment where they are self-motivating.

☐ If you don't get a high from helping people grow, stay away from management.

☐ Your employees will look to you as an example for their behavior.

☐ Learn about employment law.

☐ Interview before you hire. Avoid letting someone else do the hiring for you.

☐ Be clear about your expectations.

☐ Identify your personal "deal-breakers."

☐ It's up to you to teach your staff how to treat you.

☐ Adequately training your staff is an investment in your future and theirs.

☐ What gets measured gets done.

☐ It's your job to make your staff members feel important.

☐ Triangulation causes lost sleep and resentment.

Postscript

As with any human endeavor there will, of course, be moments of dissatisfaction, anger, and emptiness, even in the best of jobs. So long as the good outweighs the bad each day, you are probably on the right career track.

There is only one prerequisite for being in management. Above all else, you must get your kicks from watching people grow. If you are now in management and helping your staff grow is not one of your favorite activities, get out. You'll never be good at the boss business. And you won't sleep much either, because the people problems will keep you awake at night.

Dealing with obstinate employees, training, drawing clear boundaries, coaching, employee motivation, and assuming responsibility take a lot of energy. Oh, and have I said that you have to "inspect what you expect"? It's uphill all the way, but the rewards can be great.

Realize that you can't start out running the company. Allow yourself to enjoy the trip, as well as your companions, along the way. As a result of living one day at a time, you will eventually find yourself very near or even well past the goal you envisioned at the start of the journey. And speaking of journeys, success is a journey, not a destination.

Dear Jean may have answered some of your questions. If so, I am very pleased and would love to hear from you. Visit *Dear Jean* on our web page at www.jeankelley.com and sign our guestbook. Tell me what you've enjoyed, what you've learned, and what you still want to know. If I haven't answered your question here, write to me.

I can't answer your questions individually, but I am preparing a second book, *More Wisdom for the Workplace*. Please send your questions and comments to:

Jean Kelley
7030 South Yale, #601
Tulsa, Oklahoma 74136

Or e-mail them to:
dearjean@jeankelley.com

Index

TO ORDER ADDITIONAL COPIES

Contact your favorite bookstore or order below

Please send the following books:

I understand that I may return any books for a full refund — no questions asked.

Title:	Quantity	Price
_____	_____	_____
_____	_____	_____
_____	_____	_____
_____	_____	_____

Sales tax: Oklahoma residents please add local sales tax.   _____   _____

Shipping: $4.00 for the first book and $2.00 for each additional book.   _____   _____

Total: _____

Check out **www.jeankelley.com** for special discounts and other items we have available.

Fax Orders: 918-496-9153
Telephone Orders: 1-877-496-9192 (toll-free)
Online Orders: www.jeankelley.com
Postal Orders: Dear Jean Orders
                        7030 S. Yale, #601
                        Tulsa, OK 74136
                        Tel: 918-496-9192

Shipping Address:

Company Name:_____

Name: _____

Address: _____

City: _____ State: _____ Zip: _____

Telephone: (_____) _____ E-mail address: _____

Payment:

❏ Check   ❏ Money Order   ❏ Credit Card: ❏ Visa   ❏ Mastercard

       Card Number: _____

       Name on Card: _____

       Expiration Date: _____ / _____

       Signature: _____

Find us online at **www.jeankelley.com**